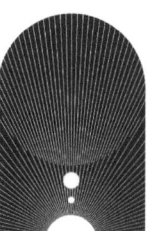

SOLUM JOURNAL
VOLUME II

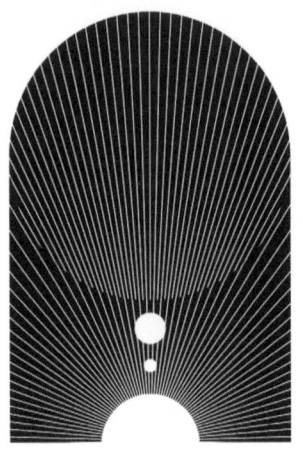

SOLUM JOURNAL
VOLUME II

AN IMPRINT OF SOLUM LITERARY PRESS

Solum Journal is a biannual literary journal. It is a project of Solum Literary Press, a Christian small press publishing poetry, fiction, homilies, and visual art.

Masthead

Riley Bounds, Publisher and Editor in Chief
Douglas J. Lindquist, Content Consultant
Matthew J. Andrews, Associate Poetry Editor
Ryan Rickrode, Associate Fiction Editor
Katie Evensen, Visual Art Editor
Sarah Christolini, Graphic Designer
Elizabeth Bristol Clayton, Social Media Manager

SOLUM LITERARY PRESS

4113 W Main St, Apt J
Norman, OK 73072
(405) 606-1997
info@solumpress.com

ISBN: 978-1-7359984-4-2

All rights reserved. No part of this publication may be reproduced in any form without the prior written permission of Solum Press editorial staff, except in the case of quotations in critical reviews or other noncom- mercial uses permitted by copyright law. For permission requests, email the publisher at info@solumpress.com with "Attention: Permission Request" in the subject line.

For submission guidelines, purchasing, and subscription information, please visit https://www.solumpress.com.

To Bart

λέγο σοι ψίλος

Contents

Call To Prayer

Michael Stalcup 1
    The Unfolding 1
Bonnie Beldan-Thomson 4
    Glory 4

Poetry

Devon Balwit 7
    Lost 7
    Ecce 8
    Bethesda 9
    No Surprise 10
Mike Bonikowsky 11
    Wildfire Sky 11
Mattea Gernentz 12
    Forbidden Fruit 12
    One for Sorrow, Two for Joy 13
    Midrash: Eve 15
    Hope 17
    Burning Bush 18
    Knowing how to swim will not save 19
    Star Shatter 20
Aberdeen Livingstone 22
    reaching out (to bridge an ocean) 22
Jonathan Chan 23
    prayer (v) 23
    advent 24

prayer (vi) 25
peace 26
wolfson chapel 27
shine auditorium...28
forgiveness 29
Jamie A. Hughes..31
Hope That Is Seen Is Not Hope 31
Into the Sanctuary 32
Apportioned 34
A Little Learning Is A Dangerous Thing.......................35
Nancy Gustafson 36
Christ's Tunic 36
Laura Reece Hogan 38
Between Gethsemane and Garden Tomb 38
Geminids...39
Hope as Alpha Centauri AB 41
Soul Nebula...42
Laurie Klein 44
Pentimento 44
Sarah Law..46
Mercy 46
Annunciation...47
Holy House, Walsingham 48
Mary Willis..49
Halfway there...49
After the Cool of Day 50
Time Out 51
A Line...52
D. S. Martin 54
El Hakabodh...54

Matthew Miller..56
    Original Sin..56
    Turned to Salt..58
    We Live in Interwoven Branches...................................60
    What Circles..61

Paul J. Pastor 63
    Julian's Wall 63
    Ephesus at Sunset..64
    Pavlov's God..66
    The Illuminated Life 73
    Telemachus Among the Suitors 74
    The Mustness 75

Dan Rattelle..76
    Evensong..76
    Abraham on Mount Moriah 77

Jacob Riyeff..78
    The Lower Narrows 78

Cynthia Sowers 80
    St. Jerome Listens to the Angels in the Desert.............80

Steven Wingate...82
    Joseph and the Swans...82
    In Memoriam Fratris...84

Fiction

Glenn Cannon...88
    Age of Igorrius..88

Elizabeth Genovise...122
    Meridian...122

Andrew Reichard 145
    Titanomachy..145

Homilies

Ryan Diaz 176
    The Holy Present..176
Greg Peters 184
    Sermon for the Second Sunday of Easter 2020 184

Philosophy

Riley Bounds 190
    The Necessity View as the Most Accurate Account of
    Metaphysical Relation in Physicalism 190
John J. Brugaletta 194
    The Concept of Evil 194

Visual Art

Cynthia Sowers 198
    Studies after Giovanni Battista Tiepolo, ...198
    Studies after Giovanni Battista Tiepolo, II 200

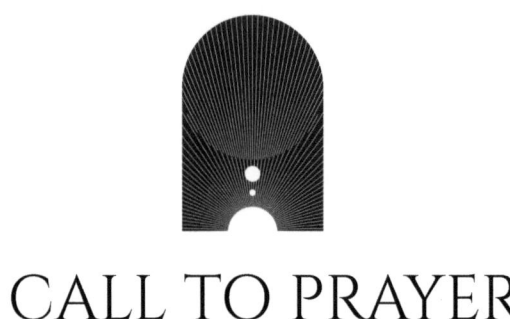

CALL TO PRAYER

MICHAEL STALCUP

The Unfolding

Each word is contained within its section's title.

Eucharist

Their Christ recast,
their hearts astir,
heirs trace his art,
etch this richest rite.

~

Gethsemane

Tense.
The stage set.
Sent as man's easement,
he sang an ashen amen.

~

Crucifixion

[INRI]
Ironic
icon: Crux of our
ruin,
crux
of
our
fix

~

Saturday

Daystar
as dust,
rays
rust.

~

Resurrection

Cinereous stone
unset—our sun
is risen!

Sin in ruins,
terror's tenure
torn,

one rescuer
incurs, inters
our curse,

returns to us
our cure, our rest,
our course.

Michael Stalcup is a Thai-American missionary living in Bangkok, Thailand. His poetry has appeared in several magazines, including *Commonweal Magazine*, *Ekstasis Magazine*, *Fathom Mag*, *First Things*, and *Sojourners Magazine*. You can find more of his work at michaelstalcup.com.

BONNIE BELDAN-THOMSON

Glory

is white,
a piling up and reflection
of all colours

opalescent water and flame,
sparkle of diamonds can scratch glass,
dark sienna of a mountain stream

shifts silver and red of spawning salmon,
strikes black rock, explodes
into white energy, the kind that made

Isaiah and Handel proclaim
"The glory of the Lord shall be revealed
and all flesh will see it together."[1]

---

1 "And the glory, the glory of the Lord" refers to George Frederick Handel's musical setting of Isaiah 40:5. It is sung as chorus 4 from scene 1 of Handel's oratorio, The Messiah.

Bonnie Beldan-Thomson is teacher and musician who lives near Toronto, Ontario. She has been writing fiction, non-fiction and poetry for a variety of publications since the mid-eighties.

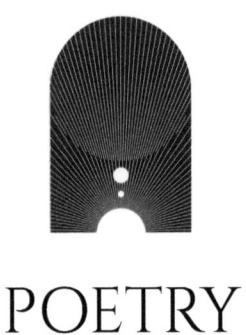

POETRY

DEVON BALWIT

Lost

I ask an old woman walking her dog
if she knows the house where the geese live.
I'm not sure I do, she says.

Do you know their first names?
Now both of us cock our heads.
I do not, I say. *They're birds.*

We pause a moment before we both alight
on long white necks, on beaks
clacking in a peaceable gabble.

No, but she will be glad to look, as I do,
each time I proceed down the block,
for this lost bit of Eden amidst the yards.

Ecce

> *(Psalm 118:22)*

The stone rejected has become
the cornerstone.

We queried on *Next Door*
and were rewarded

with chicken wire and burlap,
tomato starts and trellises.

Someone's refuse supports
our pea vines. Our worms

feast on table scraps. Daily,
we prepare the way

for an as-yet-embryonic
creation. *Quiet now,*

we say as we rescue
another cast-off thing

that with care might,
one day, bring rejoicing.

Bethesda

Year after year, I wait by the water with no way
to enter. Others emerge hale, but there's no magic for me.

My face gives me away, its yearning darkening
the already dark portico.

It's me he approaches: *Do you want to get well?*
After so long, I no longer know what well is, just the hunger

to leave this place, attracting no more pity
than any man. *Take up your mat and walk,*

he commands. Without thinking, I do, the full weight
of me burdening my soles. I walk all day

until he finds me: *Now, you are cured. Stop sinning
that nothing worse befall you.* Life looms.

Even my next meal. Afraid, I watch the crowd swallow
him up. Is it wrong to mourn infirmity?

No Surprise

He'd show 'em ...how he could build up church membership, build up the collections, get 'em all going with his eloquence—and, of course, carry the message of salvation into darkened hearts.

Elmer Gantry

When I left the church, the rector didn't call.
I didn't expect it. I'd been a bust—small
change in the collection plate, not a joiner,
an odd soul looking for salvation from the corner
pew—a Jew, no less, sneaking in
by means of old connections. I'd been
in and out before, a bad bet
from the start. Even so, I let
my empty inbox grieve me. God,
whom I was fleeing, was the only one who'd
miss me. The rector had her true flock
to consider—the regulars who didn't eye the clock
or fidget, who took on the business side
of faith and didn't need coddling to abide.

When not teaching, **Devon Balwit** chases chickens in Portland, OR. Her poems can be found in *Relief, Plough, St Katherine Review, Sojourners, Psaltery & Lyre, Presence, Rattle,* and *America* among others. Her most recent chapbook is *Rubbing Shoulders with the Greats* [Seven Kitchens Press, 2020]. Her col- lection *Dogwalking in the Shadow of Pyongyang* is forthcoming [Nixes Mate Books 2021]. For more, please visit her website at: https://pelapdx.wixsite.com/ devonbalwitpoet

MIKE BONIKOWSKY

Wildfire Sky

Come let us walk together
Beneath the wildfire sky
Into the unread pages
At the end of the story.

There is no weapon
That can defend against what comes
So let's drop our therapeutic arms
And live with open hands.

There are no tools of ours
That can mend what has been broken
So let's drop our anxious hammers
And receive what is given.

There are no words of ours
That can spell what is away
So let us shut our mouths
And listen.

Oh God, oh God, lift up our eyes
Oh God shut up our mouths
Take us by our empty hands
And lead us where we would not go.

Mike Bonikowsky lives in Melancthon, Ontario with his wife and two little kids. He works as a caregiver for men and women with developmental disabilities. In what time remains, he writes poems.

MATTEA GERNENTZ

Forbidden Fruit

I prefer to eat my clementines
before the window, letting the light
trickle in and fall with soft step across
dusty floorboards. There, I peel the rind
like a flower, a slow, holy act, sacrament
with shards spread in each lonely direction,
and I hold up every penny slice to the glow
to see if a rebel seed lies cocooned inside,
waiting to trick, to choke, to flood the mouth
with bitterness. Curse of forbidden fruit,
the beginning of the next generation or
ripe newness in death. Remove the seed.
Take and eat. Do not let it pass from me.
In not-so-tender liturgies, I glimpse light.
Heavy-handed Lord, I believe you saw
us coming, like a shadow waiting
to be born. I think you ushered us in anyway.

One for Sorrow, Two for Joy

At the Hunterian Museum,
a magpie nest, enclosed
in glass—empty. Preserved
for passerby too caught up
in the map or the museum guide
or the Egyptian sarcophagus
across the hall. I almost didn't
pause, nearly absconded
without a second glance.

Did you know that, in winter,
magpies become vegetarians?
They build their nests in thorny trees,
burrowing in with twigs-a flash of blue.
They do not migrate. Their tail is half
the length of their body. Darling, do you ever
wonder about magpies? One for sorrow,
two for joy. Bygone tradition used to entail
raising one's cap to a nearby magpie. A gesture
extended to make peace, lapsed into absence.

At the Glasgow Necropolis,
the next day, they found me.
Amid towering headstones
and mausoleums, that solvent
cyan flicker, a rummaging among
crisp autumn leaves. I wonder if
it greets or bids me beware,
harbinger of some darker order, despair.

I only wish I had a cap to raise.
Hovering betwixt vibrant totems
of life and death, I suppose
it is Eden as much as anywhere.

Midrash: Eve

Remember You are Dust

Dear one, Adam, *'adamah*,
made from your rib, your side,
it was you I did not choose
but was chosen when all things
still sang their first names,
bright like flint fire. We shone too,
radiant and ruddy, the two of us
Tigris and Euphrates, tumbling, meeting.

The antelope and ibis I nurtured,
returning at sun high, flying
across the mossy garden on bare feet,
laughter spilling like cockle shells,
to find you seated with a faraway gaze.
Quiet, you said nothing was the matter,
but I could feel a change in me: no inferior emotion,
only the yawning absence of the joy before.

Distant one, I wondered if you could see further than I,
look into the heart of some superior matter, if you could
see what was next. What did our Father say to you
before I was made? Was there some truth I missed? All I wanted
was sight beyond naïveté to protect our abundance. To protect you.

In pursuit of knowledge, I ate. In boredom, in lust,
in love, in envy, in anger did I digest. Starved, we lost all.
Our meager days reap sorrow, bleed into years,

and I survive by thinking of it—Eden,
the antelope and the ibis and the bowing ferns,
hives of bees and roses hemmed in,
haunting my dreams still. And also comes
the expulsion at the gates, and You, my Father,
turning away. Suffice it to say I no longer sleep well these days.

and to Dust You Shall Return

Hope

Found in the flicker of a newborn smile, the smell of pine,
you are the unexpected gift, long-awaited rainfall
over parched ground, every word I could not say.
You are lost time regained, both scuttling cloud and sun.
Each day, you insist on painting the dresser green,
gathering rosebuds, watching the children climb
over speckled boulders on the beach. You flee
before me without a coat—tumbling to the mailbox,
opening it with fragile hands, discovering
postcards from faraway friends and photographs
pressed with care. You are mending us even now, gathering,
dreaming our memory—the way each shadow suggests
the presence of light, the shuddering
expanse in the chest after weeping.

Burning Bush

teach me to remember,
teach me not to remember.
this fragment of Aegean sea,
housed within my breast—
premature death rattle, overturned
cup of tea, seeping. tell me
that love was made to be
bruised, a ripe fruit fallen
too soon; tell me we will not live
to regret this—the telltale aching
of our knees when the divine
passes nearby, recklessly
consumed by light.

Knowing how to swim will not save

swept away in undertow
the blessings we mumbled
circled round chipped tables,
heads bowed before the Unseen,
unaware you would arrive
in torrents, transfiguration of
the ordinary into all we could
never fathom yet desperately
awaited. even waves grow still
in memory of the dust tossed from
your sandals. even children know
flames burning brightest are blue,
o holy flame, fountain of living water.

Star Shatter

welcomed, born without invitation

entering into inevitable dance,

stumbling, beckoned further than thought,

held, awakened to the sound

of a new tomorrow, trembling.

you said "fear not."

you said "be still."

and I recall something: a not yet. so

why all this star shatter,

why quake and thrill,

why the abysmal chatter? why

Hemingway and orchids, bee

buzz and dark matter? motion

and light quickening, racing

into piercing darkness

perhaps not dark at all

but merely such brightness

we are blinded and know no more.

Mattea Gernentz is a poet and aspiring art curator from Franklin, Tennessee currently residing in Scotland. She is a postgraduate student at the University of St Andrews and graduated from Wheaton College with a B.A. in English literature and psychology. Storytelling is her passion, and her work meditates on themes of memory, nature, womanhood, and faith. Her creative writing has been featured in *The Pub*, *ST.ART Magazine*, *Kodon*, and the Institute for Theology, Imagination, and the Arts' "In/break" exhibition. You can find more of her work on her website, whimsyandwords.com, and on her Instagram page, @thewhimsicalowl.

ABERDEEN LIVINGSTONE

reaching out (to bridge an ocean)[1]

When I reach out for you
The first fumbling stretch,
The tiniest twitch of a finger
As if to bridge a vast ocean
Or pierce the atmosphere and extend into the cosmos,
Like it would take light years just to reach your outer rim—
What a surprise to make that minuscule move
And brush against *you*,
My trembling fingertips against your scarred palm,
You, right here,
Your hand stretched out to me since the day it formed me,
Your arm, the bridge over the endless void between us,
Shrinking space like an inverse red shift
To carry me home to your heart
Less than one breath away—
You, always the first to reach out for me

---

[1] This poem was originally published on the author's blog, *A Glimpse of Starlight.*

Aberdeen Livingstone is studying Religious and Theological Studies at The King's College in NYC. She loves good books, good movies, traveling, the Yankees, and her family (in no specific order). Growing up as a military kid, she calls many places home but feels most herself at the ocean or in deep conversations. She is passionate about how faith intersects with all areas of life, from art to science to daily chores, and loves to muse about them in various forms of writing.

JONATHAN CHAN

prayer (v)

askesis is like peeling
a grapefruit, thumb wedged
between pith and flesh, threads
sticking to the fingers, the soul,

that luminous thing, bruising
with every touch. that old
discipline, like the burning
off of rust, the cyclical collision

of dust and unknowing, pared
back again: does the sanctified
lie against the fragile? even if
the ethereal feels closer than

this brittle skin, delinking
chain by chain. the molecules
shift; just as that stratospheric
brushstroke peels back

a tangerine sky, just as
the trunks withstand
the gale and the shower,

just as the same glow
quivers, nothing new,
in every dusky
place.

advent

'So will I melt into a bath to wash them in my blood.'
   – Robert Southwell, 'The Burning Babe'

it begins with an aching back: the blossom
of ethereal consent, the hail mary of

morning sickness. then, the rattling of flesh
and bone, the cushioning of shit and

straw. a day of small things, not despised,
illumined under celestial gleam. and this

world: feet sent scurrying by infant graves,
the petty violence of male vanity, and the

boy-child not yet flung against the rocks.
here, beneath the undulating heat and

rain, the sweeping of scattered pines, the
piercing glare of ornamented streets, i

recall that stillness breathes
in this much cruelty. this year has been

harder to live without, this cynicism,
stubborn, for an eschatology of whispers.

prayer (vi)

by daylight, that same crawl
inward, the labyrinth of stubborn
affections, the same words that tumble
and reorder. the gap between speech and
attention yawns: the ache of straining eyelids,
the single, shuddering convalescence. again, we
must learn to chew, verse like gristle, nourishment
hard won. digestion yields its own temperance, the
fading hold of old distractions, the dissolution of
sacred and ordinary. the eye learns to hold: the
edge of a pink sundown, the silhouettes of
treetops like charred edges, the petals,
unfurling between concrete grooves,
the beams that bear up brick. i take
these truths to winter, and wait
for the blight to pass.

peace

the silence bears the restless rush of wind
across the blankness of a window's void.
the slips of paper touched and left untouched
the distant faces kept in frozen scenes.
stillness does not bristle to be heard.
the mind begins to peter into wisps:
divine echoes traced in canopies,
the slowing breaths on insulated clay;
the daybreak glittering on river spots,
the heave unquestioned, rhythm and release;
the cups of tea at spanish mountainside,
a prelude to the boundless, starry sky.
the wordless mouth can say no native prayers
but waits for all that will be said and done.

wolfson chapel

"I form the light and create darkness,
I bring prosperity and create disaster;
I, the Lord, do all these things."
- Isaiah 45:7 NIV

i have felt the urgency of prayer
by the patterns of this cell, the
faithful faces who know who i was
and will be, the life lived in widening
circles. the man of sorrows floats
in sculpted ascension, bronzed visage
of wordless plea. there is the breathless
gasp of an emptied room, yet i have,
i have turned to the touch of wistful

light, away from the fetters of sordid
baptism. the flesh tingles while suffused
in the mystery of ether, the fingertips that
brush the forehead and clarify the heart.
the pressure drains into warbling winds.
there will only ever be the presence that
breathes, the hands that quiver, the vision
that opens, and the dust that wastes away.

shine auditorium

soft light filters between
fingers held, grasping at
the edges of shapeless
glory. arms reach into
the fog, adulation funnelled
through the fingertips,
eyelids gripped by inchoate
zeal. the bodies sway,
animated by the depth of
feeling known. i feel the
rumbling: it burrows
from diaphragm through
the vocal chords, unbroken,
the heaviest breath of all,
returning to the spheres,
'YHWH'.

forgiveness
after Naomi Shihab Nye

i remember drinking deep
of that pool, the rage coursing
down the gullet, compressed
into an airtight pit. to have
been followed as prey is
to feel the palpitations under
the skin, shuddering with
every glimpse of disheveled
fury. kindness

dissolves the future in
a moment. its tender gravity
bends vascular strings, unseals
the vacuum, renews the smooth
muscle of prayer. every breath
loosens into possibility, light
through exit-wounds, the blight
of fear, hunger, the inhospitable
tarmac. and yet, it cannot bleed as
presumption. that battered body stirs
again, the turn of laced fingers:

may you know the embrace of a pedestrian
smile, may you know the calm of divine
shelter, may these words warm as an
invisible cloak, a winding peace in
scattered rain.

Jonathan Chan is a writer, editor, and recent graduate of the University of Cambridge. Born in New York to a Malaysian father and South Korean mother, he was raised in Singapore, where he is presently based. He is interested in questions of faith, identity, and creative expression. He has recently been moved by the writing of Natalie Diaz, Jamaica Kincaid, and David Wong Hsien Ming.

JAMIE A. HUGHES

Hope That Is Seen Is Not Hope

Each winter, crepe myrtle trees are brutalized
after the whiplong branches
sacrifice their blooms.
Naked and pale barked, their branches forking
like crooked arms. Gnarled fingers,
hands open to heaven morning and night.
Prayers without ceasing.

Are they lifted in praise to their leafy creator, a lipless
hosanna? Is it a plea for release as they groan
with all creation? Perhaps they, subjected in hope,
inch skyward—lamenting and pleading the case
of our shattered world,
cut short of glory and screaming.

Into the Sanctuary

I remember the wide-open space,
pews sitting outside the church
under a graceful ceiling of swaying pines,
each removed by deacons' sons
so we could replace the carpet.

I carried equipment, found outlets,
ripped up the ancient burgundy flooring,
its padding packed flat by time
and penitent knees. Rolled it tight, and
dragged it away.

I read aloud what was written above the entry:
Come unto me, all ye that labor
and are heavy laden,
and I will give you rest,
my words echoing
in the emptiness.

I opened the door beside
the now-naked platform steps,
looking for a drink of water,
and entered into hissing darkness.

Snakes, curled in their cages—
waiting for the ecstasy of handling,
to become evidence of true belief.

I backed into the exposed sanctuary
where my father and grandfather,
on their knees, worked away—oblivious.
Wordlessly walked past them
out the double doors thrown wide
to an Arkansas spring.

Down the stairs. Across the gravel.
Toward the forgiving earth. Running now
to the crooked pews in the green, green
sanctuary. Into the safety of the trees.

Apportioned

The pastor cleaves the loaf with his soft hands,
pierces the hush with its crackle.

The body of Christ, broken for you...

We come forward, receive a portion
from the proffered basket. Dip it
into wine. Leave filled.

But what of the bread that remains,
the unclaimed sacrifice?

Take it to the birds, Christ says.
I feed them, too.

A Little Learning Is A Dangerous Thing

Sometimes, I wish you'd beaten me
with a Bible, its leather-bound
chapters and verses holding me fast,
forever between damnation
and repentance.

If I could go back, I'd beg you,
knock me to the floor
with it, leave me
face smashed
into the living room rug.

At least then, I'd know
which way was up,
have an idea
of where to start walking
the path toward forgiveness.

Jamie A. Hughes is a writer/editor living in Atlanta, Georgia with her husband, two sons, and a very needy cat. She has written for *Christianity Today*, *The Bitter Southerner*, *CT Women*, *Comment Magazine*, *Ink & Letters*, *Fathom Magazine*, *The Perennial Gen*, *You Are Here Stories*, *The Brink*, *Change 7*, and *Barren Magazine*. You can read more of her writing at tousledapostle.com and follow her on Twitter at @tousledapostle.

NANCY GUSTAFSON

"When the soldiers had crucified Jesus they took his garments and made four parts, one for each soldier; also his tunic. But the tunic was without seam, woven from top to bottom, so they said to one another, 'Let us not tear it, but cast lots for it to see whose it shall be.' This was to fulfill the Scripture, *They parted my garments among them, and for my clothing they cast lots."*
    John 19: 23-24 (RSV-CE)

Christ's Tunic

I've pondered his mission
for thirty years, while I clothed
and fed him, and kissed him
at the door. Now it begins, but
    before he goes

I'll stretch my hands to the distaff
grasp the spindle, spin the flax.
Thread by thread I'll fix the loom.
My shuttle will fly
    through warp and weft.

I'll weave a priestly tunic
of linen—seamless neck to hem,
a memory of his mother's love,
the work of my hands
    against his skin.

The tunic: a garment worn next to the skin. One-piece vestments were worn by the high priests of Israel. They were woven of linen, were seamless and were never to be torn. Christ is the high priest who accomplishes his ministry on the Cross.

"Therefore, he had to be made like his brethren in every respect, so that he might become a merciful and faithful high priest in the service of God, to make expiation for the sins of the people."

Hebrews 2: 17 (RSV-CE)

Nancy Gustafson has published poetry, short stories and memoirs. She lives in Huntsville, Texas, from where she writes to express her gratitude for her life, her family, and her faith.

LAURA REECE HOGAN

Between Gethsemane and Garden Tomb

Even the blue-robed jay leans to bear
today's shining weight, raindrop

to earth. Grow stronger, not
weaker, you say. Amplify

the gardens: keep rising
through the shuddering apart of seed.

John the Baptist proliferated
in his own absence:

his decrease,
your increase.

We can only dissipate, trust
the soundless potency at root.

Even the jay disappears skyward,
leaving the faintest impression

already fading
from grass.

Geminids

Past November, past midnight,
you pull and release

whole quivers of whizzing silver shafts
into the indigo night. If I could dilate

wide enough, I'd catch
each shooting signal, let through each spark

of sight. Your words throw open
my tight shutters, spangle the black mountains,

enkindle falling diamonds,
cherished as folktales: a new baby's soul

descending, an angel in flight, the rhythmic flare
of wish and wish again—

that it might be so. That we still have time.
That you mean to give love. That pure starlight

streams the horizon. That constellations leap
across the atmosphere in a blazing embrace.

To see a waltz of Geminids, magic in the sky.
The reality is: they are tiny grains of space dust.

The reality is: so am I.
We skim across the surface of the world, dust

to dust, brief powders of fire, sure short arrows.
The reality is: eternally

we are incandescent casements
of your celestial light.

Hope as Alpha Centauri AB

Hope is not a hypothetical star. It is a luminous duo
orbiting next door, its ceaseless bright sway

of photons always arriving at the speed of light, flickering
through the fractures. Hope is not the brainchild

of a genius, a theory to span the gaps between known
and unknown facts, a frozen star to sputter a dim

prospect, a blitzar to battle doomed collapse
through harrowing gates of a black hole, or an imagined

quark star springing eternal and strange. No,
it is our nearest star, shimmering and gentle, a fiery reality

speaking to the reality which breaks through the cracks
in our nation, lives, and hurts. It is the candle on the sidewalk,

the nurse not giving up, the teacher leaving space
for the pressures of the room, the tensing future held

in the present. Hope is the binary star, the solidarity
which appears as one sure shine, steady and stirring.

It winks, precedes. It never fails to traverse the night.

Soul Nebula

You have grappled to open
the door, over

and over. You wonder
why the inside must be swept clear

so violently,
the aching cavities carved

by radiation and stellar winds streaming
from massive O stars

far too dazzling
to see. The destruction sweeps

the dark vacuum
with loneliness—yet, hollow

the nest. Empty the hidden spaces
of the glimmering nursery

within you,
forming pure new light. Baby suns

stud the rim
of waiting. Every possibility belongs

to the expansion which unlocks
the chamber, pushes wide

the portal,
sets the stars to ignite.

Laura Reece Hogan is the author of *Litany of Flights* (Paraclete Press, 2020), winner of the Paraclete Poetry Prize, the chapbook *O Garden-Dweller* (Finishing Line Press), and the nonfiction book *I Live, No Longer I* (Wipf & Stock). A Pushcart Prize and Best of the Net nominee, she is one of ten poets featured in the anthology *In a Strange Land* (Cascade Books). Her poems have appeared in *America*, *First Things*, *The Christian Century*, *Whale Road Review*, *Dappled Things*, *Cumberland River Review*, *EcoTheo Review* and other publications. She can be found online at www.laurareecehogan.com.

LAURIE KLEIN

Pentimento*

God saw it: perfectly
workable—two parts loam,
one part, play—primeval
earth, kissed

by Breath. In the garden,
Adam palmed handfuls,
day after day. The soil
settled back into his pores,
a presence, flaking away
over time, like pigment
deserting a living fresco.

To this day,
perhaps those dark molecules,
older than tremors,
retain the chafe
of his bared soles, pacing, pacing,
Adam's voice pleading,
"Swallow me."

In the falling blue dusk,
death shows its hand: How
can mere dust hope
to re-claim the original image,
and the voiceless ground cease

to lament its first undoing?
How dare Love keep breathing,

*I am alive, 10,000 times more than
Time.* Wet plaster. Paint. Our museums
showcase the Master's hand,
the priceless bleed.

> *Noun: the reappearance in aging murals
> of an underlying image, long obscured

Laurie Klein is the author of *Where the Sky Opens* (Poeima Poetry Series), and *Bodies of Water, Bodies of Flesh*. A past winner of the Thomas Merton Prize, her work has appeared in *The Southern Review*, *The Pedestal*, *The Christian Century*, *Plough Quarterly*, *Dappled Things*, and other journals, anthologies, and spoken-word recordings. She lives in the Inland Northwest.

SARAH LAW

Mercy

Neither do I condemn you. He was writing with his finger on the ground. As deserted as she – they are alone in the desert, and he engraves the scene in sand. His love is a mandala; his mercy is for sinners. The woman stands in her flame of flesh; she leans like a tulip, flushed, sappy. His shoulder sag - an invisible grief. The judges have gone, dropping their laws like stones. My heart twists the way a child hears the door. He's here: adoration bubbles up. He has saved the princess in all her wounded glory. And who's to say it was not she who later graced his feet with her perfume and her tears?

Neither does he condemn her. Their eyes meet, then her gaze drops down. He sweeps another curve into the dirt, letting their life-lines cross.

Annunciation

And the angel left her. She tried her best to stutter a farewell. It seemed tame, inadequate by nature to the task. What can one say to a departing angel, a dazzling streak of light, now she knew a halo had been cast over her whole world? She had agreed to something, agreed - given permission, said a definite yes, taken a bold first step. The sun flooded down on her like weightless honey. Her body fizzed. Her soul hummed. She put her hands together.

Later, she realised - the book fluttering at her side, the wine glass still full of water, that it wasn't a question of farewell. Quite the opposite, in fact. The angel had left her, but something remained, with her, within her. *You're welcome*, she whispered, as the air turned cooler, and the curtain gently stirred against the breeze. *Come in, come in. Please, make yourself a home.*

Holy House, Walsingham

the house is made holy with ghosts –

penumbra, shadows, liminal flickering

              striations of light   ultraviolet   infrared
green screen   blue upon blue
      emulsion of petitionary breath bound
into the hours

if your priest is squinting   he may be seeing stars   or

angels drifting   speculative
      scotoma   scintillant

despise not apparitions
      but in your mercy   that our lines be blessed
          dispensing redemption   even at the *fractio* –

indulge me: you   red rose, white light –

     are richer than wine

Sarah Law lives in London and is a tutor for the Open University. Her latest collection, *Therese: Poems*, was published in 2020 by Paraclete Press. She edits the online journal *Amethyst Review* for new writing engaging with the sacred.

MARY WILLIS

Halfway there

the water still shines green
as the shoots of mountains behind you,
green with beginnings—

does green shine through light
or light through green?

This morning sky could be the evening
in full flower,
this ocean could be opening or closing
with each wave, each petal
upright, gold-tipped.

You can see clear to the bottom,
your own precarious feet,
and feel the pull back
to hands that moved before you were born
among the roots of suns and stars
parting darknesses for you

yet stronger now
you feel the tug ahead
to where blues balance on deeper blues,
paths you will take
learning to walk on water,
finding your salvation further out.

After the Cool of Day

Light is what
we have no image of—

loss. No one else
is present

except the darkness walking,
talking to itself,
taking it for granted
we'll overhear

and trees that live
behind the names we gave them
move in when we turn our backs.

They don't know where
they came from
or why we're hiding
at home here.

Time Out

The full moon rises fast,
flicks through thick trees
as I do on a shortcut home,
running late.

Surely if I pause now
between the counter and stove,
I'll catch a rush of fire,
a flying breath

but an angel can rest
inside our world, sit still
as a candle at our bare table
so we never know it's here.

Its eye is single
and its body is all waxing light.

It doesn't waver
making a path
through things as they are
to things that may be.

A Line

The stars drift off as silently
as boats slipped from their moorings.
You don't notice
until they're out of reach or sight

and the sun has not come up yet
on its long taproot
to anchor you in light.

There's nothing to divide
your day and night.

It is a gift,
this in-between thin time
that's wrapped in blank gray paper.

You open it
by the only light left,
the one folded inside.

It is a line, a message
mailed by a persistent lover
reminding you
the lights of the world
are never enough.

Mary Willis lives in London, Ontario. Her poems have appeared in such journals and magazines as *Canadian Literature*, *The Fiddlehead*, *Poems for Ephesians*, *Ekstasis Magazine*, *Faith Today*, and *Pulp Literature*. She has published three chapbooks, and her work has been included in anthologies, most recently in *In a Strange Land* (Wipf & Stock, 2019). She has also recently completed a fantasy novel.

D. S. MARTIN

El Hakabodh
Psalm 29:3

Perceptible to the perceptive
even in a drop of water   a radiance
from well beyond each sphere of liquid
pearled on a leaf   or coursing in clouds
across the sky
           seen & unseen
a blinding brightness   or
undetectable luminescence   a shadowy shape
a subtle sound   trickling   or rumbling
or twittering with birdsong
recurring again & again   & declared
in the celestial language of stars
a mystery   shining   across the universe
& from our own sun   bold at day's end
glistening across Lake Huron   or as
understated as a grey day slipping
through the slats of a barn
sometimes brilliant   & sometimes obscured
on cloud-bound mountaintops
far too great   in its undiluted purity
for us to face unveiled
           known & unknown
the glory   of God
the God   of Glory

D. S. Martin is the author of four poetry collections, including *Ampersand* (2018) & *Conspiracy of Light: Poems Inspired by the Legacy of C.S. Lewis* (2013) — both from Cascade Books. He is Poet-in-Residence at McMaster Divinity College, the Series Editor for the Poiema Poetry Series, and has edited three anthologies — *The Turning Aside* (2016), *Adam, Eve, & the Riders of the Apocalypse* (2017), and *In A Strange Land* (2019). He and his wife live in Brampton, Ontario; they have two adult sons. Find him at http://www.dsmartin.ca/, http://www.kingdompoets.blogspot.com/, and https://mcmasterdivinity.ca/poems-for-ephesians/.

MATTHEW MILLER

Original Sin

Genesis 3

You said you didn't expect the break, not the way
a quaking aspen awaits loss

at autumn equinox. Harvesting light
from snowy chaos, shivering

all summer, anxious for the first golden
fall. Because they have no hope

that their leaves will hold, their limbs drink
sun to summon the next ones. You also said

it wasn't an instant rift, not a mountain lion's
unexpected rip through cloth and skin.

You sigh, describe the break like a hike
in craggy mountains. You believe

your child is behind you, looking
at the way you've arranged the purple sky

to catch the summit's shadow.
But they've pushed into thistles

and sagebrush, searching for cinquefoil
on the cliff's edge. Torn and teetering.

You were leading them to a meadow,
blanket flowers and buttercup, but they always choose

a ledge, where everything hangs on
the next step. They boldly risk,

creating their own pain. But, you say,
I did make them in my own image.

Turned to Salt

Genesis 19

Not limestone, which erodes like papyrus
washed over rocks or lost in the pockets

of long robes. Not even gypsum or quartz.
Not hardhearted, sharp-sided or cold, but

slowly poisoning. Marling mountains,
crumbling cups leaking salt and dirt

into fresh springs, damming them into thirsty
seas. Strangers on these shores

can't find anything to drink. So many burn
where water is deep, kneading crusts

without yeast, dry swallows. No confessions
of power, so it leeches out to surround

need. Used to ignite sulfur to drive away
snakes, now peek at their fangs, dripping jaws,

wide to bite anyone who won't run from the public
square. There, angelic light over the cliffs

reveals the shadows on the plain. So blind
with greed they cannot find the door. We turn back

into the substance of our hearts, what we secret,
what we brine. It is not death by fire.

It is a slow, half-hearted run,
legs stiff as pillars.

We Live in Interwoven Branches

Genesis 22-23

Twisted in a myrtle and juniper thicket, obstacled
by strength; horns that had grappled for to own the summit.
His snagged curves lurch and kick; prickly cedar inching closer
to his eye. One knife-like rip and he will no longer be witness
to sons dragged up blanched hillsides, the fire of sunrise, the honey-
licks of chasteberry trees and their hives. Lavender mist like lilacs.
This world of many oddities, each an invitation to find out
where we fit. On the mountain of the Lord, all was furnished for us.
Not fought for, not earned. But in the field of grief,
there's cost. The cave to bury our love, bought from strangers.
From the abundance in we trust, four hundred shekels of silver
for a snarling darkness where we hide the mourning.

What Circles

The lawnmower roams around
volunteer maples. Crowds

of urgent thoughts in my head,
like wood bees buzzing the mailbox.

Hours of a day continue in
grief. A wombed elbow

lazes around the mound
of her navel. Red pen scratches.

Children spin hand-me-down
bikes in the cul-de-sac.

The wedding ring is polished
by a bruised thumb, middle finger,

and salty tongue. A dark bird curls
through uncolored morning sky.

Stained laundry gurgles in the washer,
irises silent in the wind. I sit,

watching these years of my life
twist with grapevine.

The beliefs I've had - ones trying to end
where they began - they're burrowing,

hiding their faces from God,
leaving holes.

Matthew Miller teaches social studies, swings tennis rackets, and writes poetry - all hoping to create home. He and his wife live beside a dilapidating orchard in Indiana, where he tries to shape dead trees into playhouses for his four boys. His poetry has been featured in *Whale Road Review*, *River Mouth Review*, *Earth & Altar* and *Ekstasis Magazine*.

PAUL J. PASTOR

Julian's Wall
    Dame Julian of Norwich, anchoress, circa 1417 (May 8).

When they sealed me in,
I looked a long while
at the blankness of my fourth wall,

which became endless,
large and small
as all creation, gracious

and wholesome as nut
paste spread lovingly
on a warmed trencher, and

I saw that lath and plaster
contains all love, holds God's own
pity, welling stark

and capable, broad as
my Christ-mother, whose gentle
caul had wrapped my soul.

Then a cat leapt in
my Mass-ward window, and
eyes open, I began to see,
                      which I believe, beloved,
                      is another word for pray.

Ephesus at Sunset

1.

Alkaline song in my acid mouth,
the Christ-hymn spills, a dear free
going of words, of praise-barks
slung slobberwise, as if I am a dog
who's caught his master's scent:
you came you came you came,

and I have gone all clumsy in the tongue,
gone flop, gone adolescent in my joy, every
limb tripping every other limb

because I see a star come over the horizon
just now, a star that speaks only its own name
then mine, each syllable a prism of ground glass,
slinging light, each syllable a humming crystal egg, a snapping diode,
an alkaline song.

2.

Then I was elbow-deep in dishwater.

I looked up
as sunset light just caught
a spider on her window-web, as she
(backlit) tiptoed up her tightrope
to a sac of eggs just at the hatch, where
silhouetted like a shadow puppet

from the mahogany islands, she waved
her frontward legs, welcoming
her dear immortal young who spilled out
the worn and flattening bag, rejoicing, rejoicing,
we came we came we came,
"and this," I thought (all soapy at the wrists),
"is a type, a revelation, this" (rinsing a chipped bowl)
"is Christ."

3.

In other ages this was not known,
and even now is quite forgotten (how few
words it takes to tell the Mystery),
but it is all here, all in this first love
from which we either fall
or trip upon, trip on upward,
all us eight-legged puppies come happy to the hatch,
to our first broad glimpse of Mother-master, that star in burning web,
that maiden-cry, that blossom and that slit,
that sword dragged sharp on sidewalk brick,
that soap froth shaken in a filthy cup,
that sunset for the world, which shall turn to
our last and backward dawn:
       become become become.

Pavlov's God

Dawn in St. Petersburg. The city,
flecked with spit, digests itself.

A bell! Hear? There, under
that roof near the Institute
Of Experimental Medicine.
We cannot tell why,
but it puts us in mind
of early fishing under chilled pink clouds,
of pastry snap, of aromatic tea,
of fruit set on a tray
while a maid yawns.

The chime is silenced
by a man in silk pajamas. Soon
he washes by the heavy mirror,
sees wrinkles splay along
his eyes. Lather on the washcloth
looks like fermentation
in a glass vial
surrounded by tissue.
He brushes from his mouth
the savor of a little bile.

Later, on the street
a stranger will say *Leningrad*.
Pavlov will spit, as if in St. Peter's
sink. Pavlov will walk
toward the school—

the kennels shall be loud.
Pavlov shall again record
the moon's phase. Pavlov shall
run his tongue
over his front teeth.

***

When a bell is rung
(not that it *must* be a bell)
in proximity to food,
it will condition a dog
to salivate, even when
there is no food,
nor smell nor hope of food.

And like a spider's web, this
impulse in us is delicate and
stronger than it looks, tensile—
for there among the kennels,
as the laboratory wakes,
as muzzles yawn and stomachs
rile, atheist Pavlov with bright
and heavy-lidded eyes
hums a hymn his father sang
swinging frankincense in Ryazan, Pavlov
is swept up in desire for
the garden of tomatoes, for
his boyhood hobbyhorse
(it *did* have a little bell),

for summer swimming
under chilled pink clouds.

As dogs feed silently, Pavlov rubs his wrists
and is come nearer, to the hallway
of the seminary that withered
his belief, those friends who told
him jokes between their classes,
who asked with much unwelcome care
things like
         Ivan, what is wrong?

Pavlov leans against a kennel
yearns to feel again that the sky
is more than atmospheres
of futile gases, the earth more
than a heap of self-digesting beauty (it is a
grief that life's road runs
only toward the West).

***

Skip large now, come
with me to the to the deathbed
of Pavlov. Like the three legs
of a tripod here the disciplines cross
themselves: physiology, psychology,
and the one he will not name (long
unblinking Queen of Sciences).

Pavlov will stay conscious to the end.
Pavlov asks a student to watch,
recording his experiences. Why waste
this last experiment? And on
this bed, the great man thinks
of the dog he made with a cannula
implanted in the jaw to measure
salivation. He tries to calm
his own reflexive kicking, but
his feet seek something they once
felt beneath and disobey.

Cold, and he can't quite swallow
his own spit. Pavlov drools. He
hates (at first) this feeling of condition,
of trained happiness, this sudden stony cold
that makes alive, this sense of getting ready
for a dive, for something other than the end.

And though the month is February
and though the year is 1936
(how cold it is in Russia!)
it becomes summer in his mind, a
warmth that wends itself
beneath pink clouds between his little
gasps, that draws about his inner noise
of tuning forks, electric jerks
and twitches, now Pavlov
aches. He wants the August leap
into the purple river pool, just at the dusk,
longs for games of sticks with friends

upon the lawn, craves Mother's little cakes,
powdered with sugar
dipped in clear tea, melting—

and the great man calls to mind
(with the sound of a harmonium
grinding down among his teeth)
the personalities of all those dogs
from all his piebald years—they were
muddy pawprints in the data, a reminder
that mechanisms are complicated by consciousness.
one may be a coward, another too eager to please.
Aggressive that one, to be euthanized
before an intern's bitten. Shallow, quiet,
loyal, overbearing. Distractible, unsteady, neurotic.

The feeling of life peeling off like a suit
is indescribable. Pavlov does not mention it. There
is too much to share. He thinks of Gogol,
of the zoo just up the road where
it seemed that all the characters of *Dead Souls*
had been made animals and caged within.

(Oh, but did Serafima think more fondly
of Dostoevsky at that old benefit
than him?) Again, Pavlov is drooling, and

Pavlov's own words return:
>*I am unfortunately burdened by nature
>with two qualities.*

Yes—the old enthusiasm,
that passionate surrender, but also:

> *I am always weighed down*
> *by doubts.*

***

Now student, why does your pen
slack slowly sideways? Why do you stare
yet not know where to look?
You were chosen for your mettle,
the dark curiosity
a vivisector needs.
Write.

Record that in the gaps between
his words, the atmospheres that whistled
with his breath, great Pavlov bled
into the room's stale air images that pooled
and swirled like clouds, like sugar
powder spreading on a cup of tea.

Record that from out his mouth
came a bee with the face of a man.

Record that from out his left nostril
plumed frankincense, from his right
woodsmoke and dreams of chess
with his father by the fire, a laughing
hand set tousling on his hair,

as the king sweeps softly pawnwise
in a welcoming defeat.

Write—a feeling like dawn
came, a sense of huge movement,
as if the house were pressed by elephants, write
that in a cry, though it was silent,
there flamed up all the grief in this caged life,
all the loss and yearning without even words
for its own salivating gnaw. There flamed
all the joy, the single laugh that had echoed
every year, waxing like a summer moon,
pulling on the brain, dribbling silver
light on the last pool of the river.

Tell us what you saw, what you heard.
When the soul of Pavlov emerged
into the place that it denied,
there was a ruffle of boyish hair,
a bounding immortality, a jingling censer
shake, a stick fetched far from down
the lawn, a longing indescribable
that had been whistled home.

When it was done, there still
was the echo of

                a bell.

The Illuminated Life
    Aelred, Abbot of Rielvaulx, 1167 (January 12).

I daydream on my northward cot;
all our broad years go paging in
sweet Jesu's book. If aye, then
what wonder our margins now
sweep gauding with red birds,
woady tendrils, self-chopped trees,
wineard's antics, hunters hanging
on a rabbit's spear,
lushly-leapt menageries,
monsters, equators, all
life's swishing inks?

What wonder that our friends
pen out the Godly loves on us,
tall and gilded capitals to light
our foolscap, spell a third with Christ,
scribe in tears and bellylaughs
the canting of our lifelong psalm?

Telemachus Among the Suitors

He said, "The hole a father leaves
is empty like the space
between an arrow and
its mark: cannot you always
cut the distance once again
by half? Infinity spans the gaps
between two hairs.
It should never hit you. But
it hits you."

The Mustness

Heir of life, a broad affection
is your birthright. A compass scribing all
which furthers self in self, which does not factor
lowliness by stature or by form, but knows those
signatures which elegantly drum the core of things.
Cherish the tempos of our rumpusing.
                                                            Love:
the heirloom so obvious it may be quite forgotten,
like the joy of summer wasps, like your last name,
like outraged mint among the clover, like the dawdling
children of quick twilights, like green berries, like dull blades,
like the story scars and smiles tell, like the canny danger
each life holds merely by becoming.

Paul J. Pastor is a poet, book editor (at present for Penguin Random House), and author of several books. His poetry has appeared or is forthcoming in *The Windhover*, *Ekstasis*, *Fathom*, *Solum Literary Press*, and other fine outlets, and has been anthologized by *The New York Quarterly Review*. His first poetry collection, *Bower Lodge*, is available from Fernwood Press (December, 2021), joining his nonfiction works of Christian spiritual writing, *The Face of the Deep* and *The Listening Day*. He lives in Oregon.

DAN RATTELLE

Evensong

What saint was it who said
   that when we sing

our prayer repeats itself—
   its substance resounds

in vowels that lengthen like shadows
   in the throats of hermits

who at night could fill my abandoned
   barn of a soul

with the empty space in their howling
   Salve Reginas?

Abraham on Mount Moriah

Laughter was his name,
I'll say, when asked

or else I'll simply
wash him away

like so much
semen running

down the leg
of an unloved slave.

I'll take comfort
when it comes and sleep,

even, in sheets
away from this

wanderlust.
Call me Abram.

I'll strike my tent
and go back to Ur.

I'll leave the stars
to count themselves.

Dan Rattelle is the author of the chapbook, *The Commonwealth* (Little Gidding Press) and lives in Massachusetts.

JACOB RIYEFF

The Lower Narrows
Baraboo, Wisconsin

the Baraboo with its steep banks
lumbers thru your inviting limbs
and she is born as we are born
a passage of life and death, terrible
and bountiful at once. i passed the Fox,
the Rock and Crawfish, the broad Meskonsing
to be here with you, here at the bottom
of an ancient sea, dried up and haunting
gate to a mountain range worn
and worn by the years, by sand, by water
worn. my grandparents lived here in your ring,
one of them died here too, in earshot
of your river. but the rain drives the fog
over your bluffs and i place my hands
on wet rhyolite's ridges, hear
the hillsides singing, raindrops falling
into the swollen streams with their mournful
music. and in this gorge you place
my heart on your rocky altar, an offering
burnt of childhood and dream, clear-eyed
mortality and joy here in the narrows.
here in your shadow where the dark grey
of your sky teaches life itself,
filling the hollows, the glens. i've driven
down these roads glowing rose
and you speak to me, my kids, just as

you spoke to those before, vaunting
stone and whelming water in your wisdom.

Jacob Riyeff (@riyeff) is a translator, poet, and teacher. His work focuses primarily on the western contemplative tradition and the natural world. Jacob is a Benedictine oblate of Osage Deanery and lives on Milwaukee's Lower East Side.

CYNTHIA SOWERS

St. Jerome Listens to the Angels in the Desert

It could be the angels and their kin
who throw the sand around
(and not a wandering lion
rummaging for a bone,
or seeking a tasty toe).

Their mighty wings beat
in rhythmic waves
not far from your face, old man;
stirring your unkempt beard,
causing you to rub and blink
your elderly eyes.

Remember when those eyes saw every stroke?
Alpha, omega, tau danced before you;
and you fought for the favor
of those perplexing marks
in receptive flight across the folio leaves -
open like wings –
over the scroll – unfurling like a sail –
O pugnacious and passionate reader!

And now, a kind intelligence
guides your hand to the page
where it finds a home:
skin, dust, memory of the words

you still hear, dimly;
irrevocably:

Turn back to me, dear friend;
I remember you.

Cynthia Sowers was a Senior Lecturer at the Residential College of the University of Michigan. Until her retirement in 2019, she developed and taught interdisciplinary courses for the Arts and Ideas in the Humanities Program. Her past teaching and current creative activity is centered on the engagement of literature and the visual arts.

STEVEN WINGATE

Joseph and the Swans

Have Joseph show him the swans
God commanded the angels
and they pestered Joseph
    the ever patient
    the always busy fixing something
    the always just in time with rent
to take Jesus, still in diapers
barely learning to crawl
out to see the swans.

"Only in town for a week," Joseph
  said during lunch break while
  Mary napped at her sister's.
"Can't miss 'em." The relieved angels
  broken-spined from so much message-ferrying
  collapsed on the couch
  and shared the last beer. Joseph
  left a note for Mary on the fridge
  and slung Jesus over his shoulder
  bouncing him with each step
    the way they loved
  and saying "ba-DUM, ba-DUM, ba-DUM"
    the way they loved

until they got to the artificial lake
in the center of town. Jesus
remembered his hungers on the way

then forgot them
when he saw white swans on the water.

"Let's switch shoulders," Joseph said.
"Lots of hammering today."
While Joseph switched him
tickling the boy's belly
with his sweaty, stubbled head
    the way they loved
Jesus turned the swans from white
to black to green to white again
exploring his sense of miracle

but no one noticed
for they were all alone at the lake
and fully engaged in the tugs
and wrestles of human love.

In Memoriam Fratris

For my brother Michael
on his first birthday
without a living breathing body

I ask an extra helping
of your mercy for him
              for he had a hard life
and did not bear it well
though he came around to you
maybe
              at the end
though I don't know
because I wasn't there
because he'd kicked me from his life
and I didn't kick hard enough
to get back into it.

              Every Sunday I ask forgiveness
              for what I've failed to do:
              reaching for my brother
              in any way beyond perfunctory
              with any gesture beyond

Hey, I'm here if he needs me

              for what I've failed to do
              to the least whole of my brethren
              I've failed to do unto you.

So on this first birthday of my brother
without his living breathing body
I ask your forgiveness
for not loving him enough

        for being cowardly
        in the face of his rejection

        for being too proud to say I loved him
        until the very end. I ask

that you lift him toward you in death
and let me climb to you
                      in his shoes
when my turn comes.

Steven Wingate is the author of the novels *The Leave-Takers* (2021) and *Of Fathers and Fire* (2019), both part of the Flyover Fiction Series from the University of Nebraska Press. His short story collection *Wifeshopping* (Houghton Mifflin Harcourt, 2008), won the Bakeless Prize in Fiction from Bread Loaf Writers' Conference. His writings on faith and culture have appeared in such venues as the *Image* blog, *Dappled Things*, *The Cresset*, *The Windhover*, *The Other Journal*, *Talking Writing*, and *Belmont Story Review*.

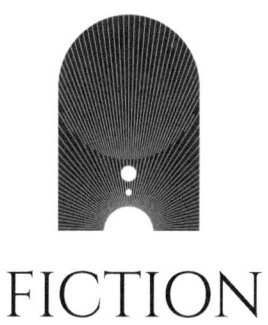

FICTION

GLENN CANNON

Age of Igorrius

Feb. 3 - I can't believe that I have finally made it out here. For so many years, over a decade, I've been promising myself I would ditch everything, get out of my little flat in the city and be with nature, for once. How is it possible for a human to live forty odd years on this planet and not experience nature? It's possible. It's designed that way.

It's only been three days, but already I am altered. This little weatherboard cabin I'm renting is comfortable, perfect. Even though the city's only an hour's drive, and I am living within the suburbs, there are times out here in the ranges when you feel you are deep in primordial wilderness. This illusion of isolation is because of the rainforest reserves all over these hills and mountains, as well as living on a steep gradient. The mountain ash gum trees can grow to about a hundred meters; the fern-trees can reach ten. When you park your car and go for a walk, five meters downhill and your car is no longer visible. A few more meters and the suburb, or village, is no longer there. Then there's just birdsong and the creak of swaying trees.

My farewell to the city feels longer than three nights ago. Dan and Gilly gave me a rousing send off. They tease me, but I think they're been supportive in their own way. I really think that. I didn't realize my break-up was that nasty until the two of them let loose on Karen after a few drinks. I caught pitying looks from them, too. A five year relation- ship – four years and ten months – ending so suddenly is a shock. I knew she was dissatisfied, but how shall I put it? I imagined her despondency was of a philosophical, existential nature, difficult to fathom. What an idiot I was. It was all based on me going "nowhere" – meaning a guy scratching out a living with bits of proofreading and tutoring work; a guy who doesn't own anything substantial, like a house, and never will.

These are the cataclysms that arrive when middle-age is suddenly in front of you, and you realize the woman you love has been evolving differently to you, has been silently recoiling from your ethos for years. I want to experience life to the fullest without hurting anything - where's the flaw in that? I thought Karen thought the same way, mostly. Actually, I thought she was more relaxed than me, that she wasn't both- ered about how we lived or the future. There were constant examples of her detachment. She was casual about using destructive fossil fuels. She drove everywhere – hated long walks, which she considered point- less. She caught planes for holidays at least once a year. She turned on the gas heater all through winter, when I thought we could rug up and endure the cold for the benefit of our carbon footprint. She was laid back about what she bought in the supermarket, whereas I had lists of taboo goods. She had no interest in embracing the discipline of my new vegan diet. She even killed mosquitos without offering quick prayers to their souls. Isn't all that a person who doesn't care too much, who just goes with the flow? But she did care. She cared that my income had stagnated, that we lived from week to week. I guess she imagined with my education and background she'd be living a better life. She saw friends and acquaintances of mine who own houses in decent suburbs and have children in good schools. Karen wanted children. I guess this became her "somewhere."

To hell with her somewhere! I'm in the right place now, among the trees, surrounded by non-human life that has no judgement, no petty ambition. I open my window – that fresh mountain air is like water to a thirsty animal. And the view! With this old cabin built on an incline, the wide sliding windows in my little living room look onto canopies and trunks of towering mountain gums and, when a strong wind gathers, the leaves roil and roar. Try telling nature it is nowhere.

I know so little about nature, a city boy like me, but if your heart's in the right place, I believe it's never too late to learn.

Feb. 5 - Was today the first day I truly and organically felt nature in its mystery and bizarreness? I think it was. This is not entirely my fault.

Our whole system and way of life is deeply prejudiced against the silent discovery, structured against the long, uneventful process of time that must precede genuine wonder and the thrill of a happening. We want nature like a highlight reel – but anyone who watches sport knows that the highlight reel, despite its quick gratification, ends up numbing you. The spectacular is only born out of a breach, a rupture, in the ordinary.

It was a nice warm day – the weather in these hills has generally been cool. I had spent hours, as I had the past few days, walking the paths through the rainforest of towering gum trees and fern-trees, my mind lost in forest murmurs and clean air, glimpsing only the occasional hiker or jogger. Then, on a quiet, narrow path, I heard inorganic music, like a machine - a keyboard synthesizer - malfunctioning, spilling wild chords in its mechanical death throes. I stopped. I stalked over to the scrub off the path for a closer look. I saw two, then three Lyrebirds – a popular motif of this region.

I hovered over a chaotic, symphonic contest between these little black birds with the long tails; these small, neurotic, flightless yet feathered ones who, like a bullied runt at school, compensate for their athletic inferiority, their inability to enter the blue yonder, with their creativity, their mimicry of what alarms and oppresses them. I figured two males had found a female and were showing off. Their repertoire was unhinged, illogical, and yet had a sick beauty that reflected everything.

From deep in their birdy throats, the diary of their lives unfurled the dubbed sounds of chainsaws, the ape-like, hyena-like bird song of kookaburras, song fragments from radio, beeping car alarms, the round and alien warble of magpies, cockatoo shrieks, lawn movers, a woman screaming in frustration, a car beeper, a car engine starting, wind murmurs, a barking mutt, other bird twitters I couldn't recognize, a jackhammer. The medley was astonishing. When they saw me these skittish creatures, like creatives jealous of their solitude, leapt and bolted for cover.

What strange inner worlds and experiences a forest must hold. What odd little, mysterious, creative, individual lives which we, in our arrogant human dominion, don't assign individuality. Nature is not beautiful or ugly. That's just human language, muck-about thinking. From stillness, life just emerges and disappears. I'm so glad I didn't have a camera or recording equipment to disfigure the experience, to share it in the highlight reel of connectivity which renders as impotent distraction everything it touches.

Power was surging through my body as I reentered my little cabin. But soon, after sipping my coffee, I became troubled. So much of the lyrebirds' medley sings of human encroachment. The towering eucalypts and fern-trees, the wondrous talents of its dwelling beasts, why are they so great yet so powerless? If only they had some form of natural resistance against us, then everything would be fine, everything would be in equilibrium, but what can resist the brutal logic of a species with our ambition and desire to get "somewhere"? Soon, the little spirit of the lyrebird will be totally annexed. Its song will be nothing but machine noise, human noise. What a travesty that would be. That's what these little birds unconsciously told me. Unconsciously? I guess that has to be the case.

Feb 6 - Slept like a log. A night's sleep like I haven't had since childhood, where your head hits the pillow and then you open your eyes into the light of day thinking someone is playing a trick on you, but no, nine hours have passed in a second.

Feb 13 - And just like that a week goes. I don't know if being away from city life will recharge my batteries or deaden them forever. I've been sleeping ten hours in twenty-four; fitful sleeps with odd dreams. I fill my days with basic household chores plus collecting and chopping wood.

Every day I spend hours walking. I go on long, meandering walks to the local village, detouring there and back through the forest reserves. Aside from people serving me in cafes, the local post-office and the local convenience store, I've interacted with no-one. At night, I muck around on social media - flicking and twitching at this and that - and wallow in the nostalgia of old TV shows and the grooves of old songs.

Though the wilderness is all around, as you walk off the main roads and forest parks, you find housing everywhere and new builds. There's money up here. Some of the houses are huge. There's a peculiar quality to these mountain/hillside suburbs. I feel I could live in my cabin for decades and not know what happens in any of these nearby houses. I could walk endlessly by them and never be invited in. At least nature's house in the forest welcomes the stranger. The fern-trees, who have been here from earliest time, never complain when you enter their domain. I sense (or is it only hope?) that one day, like with the lyrebirds, something will happen on one of these walks of mine. Life, mystery, will break-out before me.

Feb 15 - Walk to village along road. Café and paper. Eat. Walk through forest. Afternoon nap. TV. Fire and noodles. Social media distractions and television nostalgia. Sleep.

No door unlocks. No new vista. Around that corner, cut across that glade through the forest - a person, a place, something ... What? I didn't make my brains to think. I didn't make my eyes to see. They happened. This force that made me happen, please propel me towards something.

Feb 19 – Nothing ... just round the corner – nothing. But there is something. A heaving; the forest is mournful, but profound. Yes, the forest is wounded. No ... not what everyone thinks ... not just environmental destruction. It's that the human heart has turned from it. We have shunned its music, its texture, its company. We can't communicate with it. We prefer our distractions. Even the best intentioned ones politically – many like me – only love it in the abstract. But the forest lives. It wants our hands and feet to love it purely – devoid of stiff morality. The forest is heavy with betrayal and defeat. It cannot gain the undistracted, undivided attention of lived, everyday love, the real kind - devoid of sugary, highlight-reel specialness. And I mourn with it; but guiltily, like a traitor, in my gathering boredom.

Feb 22 - The mournful forest has slumped shoulders. Kookaburras mock the depressed spirit, erupting in malicious laughter at the anxious human face. The cockatoos tell a song nihilistic with growling tedium. I could walk myself to death and never grasp the wisdom of nature. I could, at best, only attain the madness of these shrieking, giggling, flying things, which seem to me the soul of an unhinged God.

Feb 24 - Walking. Nothing. Nice weather. Feb 25 - Nothing. Wet.

Feb 26 - Nothing. Wet.

Feb 27 - Nothing. Walk and eat.

Feb 27 – Still nothing. Hang out washing; won't dry.

Feb 28 - Nothing. Threw this diary in recycling bin this afternoon, but fished it out in the evening.

Feb 29 - Nothing. Walking. Legs achy. Nothing.

March 1 - And then life broke across me. Something. I tell myself it's all hocus pocus – and yet. I've been staring at this picture all day, on-and-off, from late morning till evening. I found myself mesmerized, melting time. It's beside me on the desk; it's as clear as day. The intru- sion is there. It hovers over me. It yearns to be at one with me, to share its wisdom and its pain.

This morning, I was walking through a bit of forest maybe an hour or so from my cabin when I decided to detour off the track through the scrub. I've been doing a bit of that, getting more adventurous, orien- tating better, feeling my way through labyrinths of tall wood, watchful of all the nooks and crannies in the low growth in case of a snake hole. For a moment, I was lost and I panicked – I didn't have my phone on me – but finally I noticed the trees stopping in silhouette against a horizon of light, and then I heard choppy chords from a brass band.

Some kind of fete or market was on in a nearby village. I climbed down the bank on the forest's verge and crossed a road. In front of a municipal building was a broad, gravel parking area set up with market tents and various open stalls on trestle tables. A moderate crowd was milling about, going in-and-out of the municipal building where the band – mostly retirees - was tuning up by the entrance. Nearby was a football oval, a picturesque sward of green with a nice old wooden pavilion. Here a kid squealed; a dog barked. A haze of clean, civic, family fun hung over everything. The day was fresh, clear and pale blue.

I distracted myself among the little stalls which sold second-hand books, jams and pickles, honey and related bee products, more books, second-hand clothes, second- hand shed-stuff like carpenter planes, hammers, garden implements and the like. There were old typewriters, pots and plants, odd bits of electrical equipment – antiquated – six- foot- tall wooden sunflowers, a store full of new-age stuff like crystals and incense and so on. I drifted with the crowd in circle after circle, wanting to participate and yet not wanting any junk. I ate a nasty samosa and had a surprisingly good coffee. Then I went inside the municipal building.

There was a smorgasbord in the main hall. Many elderly people were sitting about, eating and chatting. I doubled-back down the corridor which led off to two smaller rooms. In one were all sorts of books, pictures and memorabilia related to the hills. In the other, people were lining up to have their photos taken. That was curious.

The kind of photo being taken was something I last saw as a youngster at a fete. They were so-called "Aura" pictures, the type that capture the electromagnetic field around a person, like a colored halo. The younger people there seemed excited, comparing the different aura colors in their portraits. I hung around; I figured the ten dollars for the photo was for the bushfire appeal, anyway. Before long, I was standing against a silver-white background in front of a photographer and his contraptions: A rectangular box camera hooked up to a couple of flat, square, metallic objects. There was also a printer and a lap-top.

I stared into a little red light as instructed. Then, when the guy responsible for the photo said "Ok, ready?" the noise of a chainsaw revving up and cutting rumbled through the building.

After a bit, a young lad handed me an A4-sized envelope. I took out the photo in the corridor and had a look. My aura was big and green, but above and behind my head was a sharp red crescent, like a sword or a scimitar, which from the momentum in the color distortions looked like it was about to slice through my head.

I was staring at the shot when I became aware of a man hovering over my shoulder. As I exited the building this man called out: "You're a sensitive, brother."

Outside, I turned to face him. I recognized him as the vendor of one of the market bookstores. He was about my age, with a full shock of shoulder length, grey-streaked, brown hair and a handsome, swarthy, full-boned, gypsy face. His slightly frayed clothing – shirt and tie, slacks and a tweed waistcoat - had a grungy flair that comes from creative op-shopping. He had various trinkets and amulets around his wrists – of cloth and metal - and his fingers and ears were heavy with all kinds of rings. The chainsaw whined again, then stopped.

"Hey?" I responded.

"You're a sensitive brother," he said, over chirpy, like he'd done a few lines of speed. "Swoosh! Grrrrr. Grrrrr. Grrrrr. You took it deep in your aura. The green, man. You feel the green. And you're on a blood high. You know the song? Don't know? It doesn't matter. You're looking at me so seriously!" He patted my shoulder. "Chill out; we're all friends here. I'm a sensitive too, but sometimes my girlfriend doesn't think so. Ha, ha. That's a joke. Are you cool? Sometimes we sensitives can get het up," he blathered. He introduced himself and we shook hands.

"So, you're a sensitive guy, huh?" he said, looking me up-and-down as if some other authority had pronounced that judgement. "All shapes and sizes, evidently! Ha ha."

He rambled on with a glint in his eye; he tugged his hair back into a momentary ponytail, and widened his eyes pretending he was scared of me. I've been told I have a tendency to scowl. He seemed to be having fun.

"What do you mean a sensitive?" I asked him, finally able to edge
in a word.

"The cut. Come on, you saw it. Your eyes nearly popped out. I was watching you watching it and it's all watching us." He widened his hands, opening his palms to the surrounding forest and the sky. On-and-off, the chainsaw whined and stopped. Again, he patted me on the shoulder. "Chill, man!.Chill of recognition, maybe? It's out there, feeling. There are the scientific facts if you're interested. The forest feels. This isn't some hippy shit – hey, I love hippy shit - I am hippy shit! - but this is science. We're all connected, breathing each other; it's all oxygen, carbon, nitrogen flowing through each other. It's everywhere; it's why you felt the chainsaw in your aura. You heard it. It sunk its teeth into you a bit, did it? You got the forest empathy."

"What does that mean?"

"The sensapy. The sensitive empathy. Did you feel it in your body? The forest gets nervous, scared by the chainsaw; it sang out to you, cut up your aura. Big red slash."

"I felt nothing." He had to think.

"You think you felt nothing, but you felt something. Your aura doesn't lie. No two aura shots are identical. It comes from your body magnetism, and the body doesn't lie. I knew I'd meet someone today. Are there a lot of fives in your birthday? Five's my number. I see it everywhere."

He's a maniac, I thought. He insisted I go over and look at a book he had, all the while raving about the numbers on the car plates that day all adding to five, multiples of five, numbers in sympathy with five, drawing links with this to our mutual 'sensapy' all confirmed by my birthday numbers, a couple of which he cherry picked to add to fifteen - a multiple of five.

He went behind the new age stall. Obviously, he and the pretty young woman running it were together. He rummaged about then went over to his adjacent table of books holding towards me a worn out paperback, motioning me to come over. He waved the book about as he talked.

"Plants feel things, man," he declared. He had a huge smile and, as ludicrous as he was, I couldn't help warming to him. "You've got to read this book! I'm only selling it because I've got another copy."

He went on about numbers again, peppered his talk with rapidly read fragments from his book, told me he played the harmonica, mentioned his mistreatment as a child before launching into a diatribe against phone towers and humanity's mistreatment of bees. He was one of those guys who manage to be crazy and make some sense at the same time.

"I'm rambling I know. (Don't look at me like that!) Okay, so I'm not an authority, but this book is."

He put it into my hand. It was titled, "The Secret Life of Plants." I listened more to his mind spasms. As batty as he was, I could see that this man was a stranger to malice and, appropriately, I bought the tat- tered old book off him (its spine is broken) for ten bucks – two lots of five - to mark the beginning and end of our brief friendship.

March 3 - I've been reading the gypsy's book, my book, and I keep coming back to the same question. Can a person of reasonable intelligence, living a full life, go into their grave without any knowledge at all of the basic facts of their existence? Can you, at the end of it all, have no comprehension that a nose was attached to the end of your face? I wonder.

I recollect another book I read ages ago that got me thinking. It was a book about meditation written by a man in his mid-seventies who had started meditating after turning seventy. He came to the real- ization … after the age of seventy … that he hadn't been breathing correctly. All along. It took him seven decades – a professional bloke, a leader in his chosen field - took him seven decades to work out how to breathe!

It's everywhere. Here, a highly-educated, professional type figures out they've been sitting wrongly for fifty years. Another, that they've been brushing their teeth wrong, likewise, for half-a- century. And the most embarrassing thing of all is that I might be kith and kin to these snail people of the intuitions, these muddle-headed urbanites.

I guess I never thought about plants. Of course, I don't believe everything in this book. There's stuff in here about the transmutation of elements that must be junk. And yet … it can't all be untrue. Like all those paradoxes in physics, there are mysteries still.

Here's something of what I've learnt:

By putting electrodes on leaves and connecting these electrodes to a machine, electromagnetic reactions in a plant can be verified and monitored. Similar to the aura I gave off in my photo, all living things give off these electro-magnetic waves. The machine with its responsive needle (similar to ones in a polygraph or lie detector), can chart the plant's reaction to stimuli.

In one test, when a researcher went to cut a plant's leaf, the needle on its chart went haywire. It didn't go haywire at the cut – but at the researcher's intention to cut. Can this be a form of floral telepathy? Can it be operating all around us? In another test, two similar plants, I forget what, were growing side-by-side – call them "A" and "B". "A" was all wired up to electrodes and the machine. "B" was uprooted and chucked into boiling water. "A's" chart went haywire. Are there feel- ings there, empathy? And these tests aren't done by hippies or gypsies. Even Russian scientists back in the old USSR were up to it, wondering at remarkable ways to bolster their agricultural output. Would they indulge in some nonsense utterly devoid of scientific merit?

I just wonder. The leafy, blooming ones, whose twisted feet live beneath the soil, whose little souls are so dedicated to the worship of light they yearn only to go up, and up - they love classical music! They grow better with it. Can it be? Yes, I'll admit it, I'd heard this before, but we can hear things without hearing them. Like when you hear 'all people die' – a platitude like that - you feel nothing. Then one day, this boring old truth enters your psyche like a monster. The spectacular, the outlandish, explodes out of the mundane.

March 4 - I have read many more marvelous things in my little book. The most stupendous - a researcher and his philodendron plant created such a psychic bond that when the man got assaulted in an alley one night, he took note of the time afterwards, trudged home, all bloodied and bruised, and on the chart that his plant was connected to, he saw a distressed wave period corresponding to the time of his assault - a con- vulsion of rapid up-and-down strokes lasting three minutes, mirroring the attack's duration and turbulence. How? The man was miles away from his plant; he was hooked up to nothing, and yet the empathy of his vegetative friend was able to reach its leafy little soul right across the city and suffer with its master.

Master? But maybe not master. One wonders who the master is when our chlorophyllic siblings possess such remarkable gifts.

But at the end of the day, my little book is just a collection of other people's testimonies. I have to get down to business and conduct my own investigations. Tonight, I'll meditate on it and make a plan, formulate the procedures for an experiment to confirm for myself whether there's any sentience going on around me in the photosynthetic realm, or if it's all just new-age baloney. In the morning, my experiments will begin.

March 5 - Here then are the bare facts of my experiment, begun ear- lier today, to confirm once-and-for-all-for-myself the sentience or lack thereof our greenly kins-beings, if kins-beings they be and not just unfeeling matter. I decided to avoid the well-worn paths of direct phys- ical cruelty in science, it seeming to me monstrous to lacerate live plants or to fling them into boiling water just to prove they have feelings. I decided on a more psychological approach.

For my experiment, I selected two relatively young fern-trees at the bottom of this steep property, down by the creek. I decided on two ferns about my height, as my intention was to speak directly at them. Though the property is covered with them, finding such trees isn't as easy as it sounds. Whenever I spied one I thought was about my height, I realized on moving closer that its trunk might've been, but, with the way its fronds cascaded upwards, the tree itself was way over two meters tall. But, finally, I found a couple more-or-less the same height as me, and in more-or-less the same condition as each other. I took photos of both in order to have a comparison point later on. They were also at opposite ends of the property, about forty meters apart, which suited my purposes. My experiment, based loosely on one in the book, was the following:

To one fern I said wonderful, loving things and to the other fern I said hateful, threatening things. In order for there to be consistency over the duration of the experiment, I wrote down the two different texts to be read out to Fern "A" and to Fern "B". If they are such feeling, sentient beings, then the psychological should impact on their physical well- being. As an additional note, while I was delivering these panegyrics and maledictions, I lightly held the frond of the plant I was addressing, so that it would know I was addressing it personally, there being so many plants in this forest.

Here are the loving words and cadences of praise I heaped upon Fern "A":

O fern. Your beauty - natural, giving and gracious - makes every human achievement seem second rate. Even though there are mil- lions of ferns like you in this forest, you're a special one in your own right; no doubt about that. And I want to tell you a secret that I hope you'll always have in your soul: we humans, no matter what we shall ever achieve, are nothing without you. That's a fact. You are the very air of our lungs; you enrich our soil; you create the eco-systems that make us possible; every achievement of the human, whether it is space flight or playing violins, owes its birth and existence to your primordial life force. You are more original than us, indigenous to this land, an ancient force, favored by the Gods with innocence and subtlety, with the most beautiful characteristic of all in the universe, absence of vanity. You are, in your soul, immaculate in your unwavering loyalty to the pure elemental truth of Mother Earth. When she depletes, your per- fect, integrated empathy makes you suffer with her; whereas we humans, well … if we get a job promotion we rejoice even while the ecosystems are devastated. We're psycho. We're nothing next to your pure intuitive wisdom – the way you know, always will know, always can only know, that clean water is good, light is good, growth is good.

"You never stray from the deep intuition of such truths, O pure being – in this lies your beauty which makes me want to weep. Only you have remained true to Eden's original, biblical purity. We should be learning, all of us, daily from you, and yet … we humans commit the embarrassing sacrilege of destroying you throughout the world. No, you are not beautiful – I was wrong – you are beauty itself, and we're nothing without you and we should never, ever, forget it."

After those effusions of love, I trooped over to Fern "B" to orate the following:

You indigenous fuck-face! Look at you, you pathetic excuse of an imbecile vegetable kingdom fuck-face! Victim! You know I could chop you to pieces right now if I felt like it, because you're so pathetic. You can't move! Not like me – suck on that! How can you be like that for millions of years, you dickhead, and never even evolve the desire to walk about? You know if a human calls another human a vegetable it's an insult? That for us is a fate worse than death, you insensate halfwit. Do you even have a sex? How do you fuck? Through the air with anyone? Fucking pervert! Birds shit on you, and you're grateful for it. Fuck you! You think it's so fucking great to be green and serene out here - I'll set you on fucking fire - see how serene you are then, moron. I'll chop all you mother fuckers down and build a fucking tennis court out here – have a good bourgeois time on your fucking corpse, you fucking idiot plant. What do you think about that? Look at you - a great mop of green hair on a fucking stick. That's life? Get fucked! Can you draw? Can you? Can you play a bit of bass guitar? Can you do algebra? Can you build a shelf? I can! Can you do anything at all you worthless, photosynthetic cunt! Can't go anywhere, can't do nothing, at my mercy - fucking inferior life form. You make me puke. Sentient? Get fucked! You're compost. You rank lower than what comes out my ass every night!"

Such was the deranged abuse and malediction that I forced myself to spew at Fern "B".

And later in the later I repeated these disparate effusions.

I will keep this experiment up for a week, twice a day, and take photos of the ferns to track the effects. Hopefully, none of the other renters in the other cabins will - if they walk along the creek – hear any snippets from these experiments. The scientific nature of my behavior would be misconstrued.

March 6 - Took photos of both fern A and B before continuing with panegyric gushings for A and unhinged hate rant at B. Went for a short walk. Watched the "Rockford Files" on free to air TV in afternoon. What a decent, capable man Jim Rockford is; what a sense of nostalgia I get to watch things that existed as I was just entering this world; to hear theme music which accompanied my earliest breaths in this world. What a strange longing and sadness you get from watching these old shows, a mourning for once vigorous faces now very old or passed. Looked at old photos of me and Karen from happier times.

Did various life-sustaining necessities regarding my own biologic function; for example, ate baked beans out of a can, on toast – before re-entering garden in late-afternoon to deliver another hymn of praise and subsequent tirade. Continued with photo record. Among other things, collected and chopped wood for indoor fire. Nights are colder now. Made pasta. Alternately watched TV, computer and fire.

Every year my friends grow older and more apart; with internet pictures we are complicit in making lurid tapestries detailing our physical decline, half-smiling our way towards grey flesh.

Surely the Bionic Woman is pre-eminent among TV beauties from the 1970s.

Am interested to note fire, computer and television are entertaining in their movement and changes, but fire entertains with a complete absence of nostalgia, of lingering sadness. A grand principle of nature is change without sentimentality. So the forest feels no sentimentality towards us?

March 9 - Keeping up my twice daily experiment - my oration of great warmth, and my paroxysm of demented abuse. Recording vegetative response with photos. Maintaining personal biologic functions throughout. For example, did and hung out my laundry and drove to a nearby town- ship to do shopping. My walks are shorter. Watched old TV shows (varied/random times of day and night). Shows are anything from twenty to nearly sixty-years old. Comedy or drama - there's nothing deliberate in them that interests me. What fascinates is the sense of death that hangs over a surface of image and sound so full of life. That beauty is seventy-seven-years-old now. That robust dude died ten years ago. But the trees just sway indifferently and the fire in my hearth burns unconcerned.

Cannot verify for sure any changes in ferns A and B by looking at phone pictures. When I stare at them long enough, I manage to convince myself fern B – sufferer of my rabid castigations - is looking worse for wear, but this could just be me projecting. Results aren't clear.

March 12 - Now I'm convinced. The past few days, I continued much like the others, only increasing the tempo of my experiment to three sonnetic effusions towards fern A and three shrill invectives towards fern B. Then this afternoon, simply looking at them from a distance, I saw without a doubt fern B was worse for wear; it is yellower and browner, its fronds tattier than fern A. Still, to be professional, I peer reviewed my findings. Firstly, I sent pre-experiment photos of both ferns to Gilly and Dan and asked them which looked better. After side-stepping a few of the questions and smart-ass comments they texted, it was clear they couldn't spot the difference. Then I showed them the latest photos, being careful not to reveal details of my experiment.

"Looks crap" and "looks pretty fucked, in comparison" were the descriptions they texted back for Fern B. "Seems healthy" and "much better than the other one" they said about fern A.

So it is confirmed! It is unbelievable. They have feelings! The forest is alive in ways that are beyond standard human understanding – and most abominably, I sense we've known this all along.

I went and apologized profusely to fern B, telling it I didn't mean all I had said, and that it should be proud of the role it has played in my meta-physical, scientific and holistic verifications and conclusions. And then I gave it the soothing spirit balm of reading to it all I had composed in praise and lovingness to fern A. I hope this little green-haired stump of a fellow, this woody little damsel, will forgive me.

March 13 - Jesus Christ! Day began as-per-usual. I had a coffee, some jam on toast, and then by habit went down the property towards the ferns. I gave fern A a pat, told it that even though I would no longer continue with my tender hymn of praise it should remember it was a special being, and then I moved off to fern B. But where was fern B? I couldn't find it. I even wondered in a kind of delirium if perhaps fern B, feeling bru- tally used and violated for experimental purposes, had uprooted itself in protest and left the property in disgust. Of course that was absurd. I calmed myself. Then I took all my markings and angles and there was no doubt about it – the emerald green fern standing before me with great fountains of fanning frond hair was fern B! I couldn't believe it! It had taken one short pouring of kind words to utterly reverse the damage inflicted. Let it be said that nothing moves more swiftly than these still ones, these chlorophyllic parables. And what is true of the ferns must be true for all plants to greater or lesser degree.

I am not a religious man, but I felt a wave of awe and had a desire for prayer. The urge to throw myself down on my knees was overwhelming, so I did. And here's what I said to the towering woody kingdom encir- cling me, to the whole forest of ferns and gums and everything else that is in it and of it:

"I wish you could tell me something of your feelings. I know now you are sentient. I am not a scientist; I don't want to cover you with elec- trodes and study and chart you, to figure you out in that cruel human way of ours. When we humans figure things out there's always misery - you can be sure some rat somewhere has had its eyeballs ripped out, some monkey has been flung into outer space, some greenly one fed a steady diet of poison. I will not dictate how you communicate with me, so let me invite you into my psyche directly. Show me what you are. Show me what I am. Show me what you want to show me, O fellow sentience … and not what I fabricate to hunt.

"O megaflora! I empty myself for your approach! Reveal yourself to me you nameless wonder! You who have never left the stronghold of Eden's spirit; never been lost in the knowledge of self that … gives birth to the human ego and a million-and-one fantastic disfigurations and laments …that …"

And then, just as these heart-wrenching proclamations were splut- tering out, and I was groping for even grander words, my phone went off.

For a spilt moment, in a kind of delirious ecstasy, I thought I would hear the voice of the forest on my phone.

But no, it was Dan. He said he'd come visit tomorrow. Perhaps a little human company wouldn't go astray.

March 14 - It has spoken. What was said? What was the nature of it? What kind of entity is it – one empowered by the forest, or something greater? It's beyond speculation.

Dan came; I've known him for thirty years. Who is he? He has never performed in that way – and yet there's no doubt I saw the real him. He came from the other side of the city, over an hour's drive, and arrived here late morning. The weather was mild. I showed him round the property. He was normal in the beginning, maybe more high-spirited than usual. I assumed it was the mountain air; it affected me that way at first. He was amused by my rural circumstances, my shack among the gum trees. He knows I've always been an urban guy.

"Get away from people. That was my advice. This is your response!" he joked, laughing, as he gaped at the towering forest all around us. As I've said, where I am looks more isolated than it is, but first impressions can be powerful, and I started laughing too. I felt happy.

We went into my little sitting room, sat by the window looking onto the towering trunks and descending leaf canopy of the mountain gums. We sipped our coffees and caught up. The weather turned, as it can so suddenly up here; the sky whitening; a gust hitting the trees.

As we chatted, the trees began roaring in the background, and slant-ways rain spat across my tin roof and balcony. A distant cockatoo barked. I noticed Dan staring into my unlit fireplace in a kind of trance. After the passage of some time, he declared in a strange whisper, "No, way you could chop wood better than me." Why he said that in such a serious tone, I couldn't guess. It had no connection with our previous conversation, which was friendly catching up. I pretended not to hear him.

The living room became loud with the roaring of the eucalypt canopy, its leaves clapping like millions of frenetic hands, delirious with joy at the approaching squall. A small branch clanged and scraped across the roof. Dan gazed at me as the rain picked up intensity.

"Look at the thickness of my forearm," he said, leaning across his armchair to stick his great meaty, hairy forelimb into my face. We were more or less opposite each other, his back to the window. He held his arm there, must've been thirty seconds, more, for me to appreciate. My arms are quite skinny.

"I can chop wood much better than you," Dan persisted.

"I don't doubt it,' I replied. Dan really is a burly guy. He was quite the high-school athlete and, even though he's past forty, he's still as strong as a bull.

"How can you just say that to me that way?" he asked, fixing his pale blue eyes on me. I was startled.

"Say what?"

"Concede like that, that I would chop wood better. Why wouldn't you argue that point?"

I didn't know what to say. We sat quietly as the rain deluged white sparks on my balcony, and the forest transformed into a giant pompom, the swaying trees like crazed cheerleaders hailing the arrival of an outlandish spirit.

I decided to do something; I got up and started the fire. When I sat back down, Dan stared into my face, still demanding an answer to his weird question.

"Because I don't doubt you would chop wood better than me. Why would I argue a point I couldn't win?"

Dan, gesturing slowly with his hands, seemed to be addressing the flames in the fireplace that had gathered in a burst thanks to the dry leaves and bark I put in with the kindling.

"But when you concede a point so quickly, what you're really saying is that contesting the point is beneath you." He slowly turned behind him to look at the turbulent forest. Looking out that window, it was like we were driving through a gigantic car wash made out of leaves.

"Yes, I suppose," I said, feeling heavy and numb. "I don't care about chopping wood. I don't particularly esteem prowess in such a thing."

We fell silent again. Then Dan demanded: "Where's your chessboard?"

After rummaging through my bedroom – much of my stuff is still in boxes - I found my old wooden, transportable board. We moved from the armchairs to the higher table, where my computer is and where I eat my meals and write this diary. I cleared a space, feeling the roaring forest had its version of electrodes stuck on us, dissecting our friendship.

The chessboard struck me like an alien object: abstract and human; brutal and absurd. After a few standard moves, with neither of us establishing a better position, Dan orated, his voice distant and earnest:

"The world will sigh its collective relief when I, step-by-step, establish my dominance over you in this game. Already, I have defeated you physically with my thicker forearm in a forfeit – and work built my forearm, it's not illegitimate, designer gym-muscle. So let us never forget the victory of my thicker forearm. And when I checkmate you, you'll have nowhere to hide because I'll have ass smashed you intellectually as well. Oh, I know, I know, you'll then try to laugh it off with a cultural victory - as you do - by cooking up, one day, a superior spaghetti Arrabbiata with the appropriate wine, but I just want you to know that I know what that meal is all about, that I'm all over it, and that even if it comes with excellent, home-made garlic bread, no force on earth, cultural or otherwise, can negate my victory. The world will sigh its collective relief."

I started giggling hysterically. I wanted the entire forest to smash through the roof and obliterate us.

"Fuck you're a funny man," I said through my unhappy laughter, straining for breath. Dan's face was pale and immobile like he was sleepwalking.

"What's so funny?" Dan demanded in a monotone, and now his look unnerved me. Over his shoulder, obliquely, I could see the tem- pest crashing through the branches. Oh, it was speaking! Through the auras that bind us all, some kind of truth serum had been put through poor old Dan.

"The world will sign its collective relief, will it, man? when you kick my ass in a game of chess," I quoted back at him. "Do you think anybody cares about a game chess between you and me?" Dan didn't seem to register what I said.

"You look at my structures, the way I use my diagonals, the way I coordinate my attack and defense. Throughout this world, how could anyone resist my subtle intentions?"

I was stunned. "But what about reality, man?" I countered, plodding with my thoughts like I had to make ground against the gale outside. "Plenty of people could resist your subtle intentions. The fact is, we're men of moderate skill in this game. A gifted child could beat us easily. Remember, as students, all those years ago, when we dropped into the university chess club to try our hand? We were easily beaten by the club's lower-ranked players. Of course; they've got books everywhere about how to play – texts and games of the masters - they study for years. Of course our skill level is low - have you forgotten?"

Dan stood up and moved over to the fire, picking up the iron poker and making adjustments, adding kindling and a small log. He put the implements down with a slow, deliberate motion. He stared through the window at the blur of forest then turned to me, pinching his brow.

"But those guys at the chess club," he said, taking an armchair and talking into the fire while I watched from an oblique angle behind him. "I have defeated them every day with my driving skill, my superior stick-shift dexterity, without them even knowing it. You know, I'm sur- rounded by idiots. Are you aware that as a qualified electrician, I under- stand, inside and out, OHM's law, among other achievements, like being a registered builder and being one of the better architecture students before I dropped out of that piddling middle-class course? Did I men- tion I understand OHM's law? There's circuitry humming all around us, and yet out of you and me, it's me who understands the principles of resistance and voltage pressure. With my tools I harness it - you don't know how. Perhaps those wankers at the chess club also understand, but what can they do about it? I can do and act. Even your roof, I can put a new one on easily. I just rip the old one off and use it as a template, trace over the top and box gutter it myself. Even after six lessons only … only … compared to all yours, I was better at tennis than you. My backhand was better. Are you aware of my better innate understanding of slicing the ball? Are you aware I was runners-up at javelin in the associated schools of Victoria athletic carnival? Of course you were, and yet you won't pay fair respect to my achievements … and look, just look at the flames here I've got in your fire! Just look at it! I sensed the aeration need and tweaked the edifice structured upwards to allow for air flow. Can't you see all this entitles me … entitles me … in ways you can't imagine? Why your Karen didn't suck my cock at my first introduction to her is ridiculous … one of the universe's great injustices."

I was cradling my forehead in my hand.

"Geraldine," Dan said softly, still looking into the fire, referring to his girlfriend and mother of his child, "has a better ass than any woman you've ever been with."

At a higher volume Dan added, while lifting and turning his head for my benefit, "My profile is nobler than yours even if I didn't finish my degree and you did. But I love you man. I'm the best friend a man can have; a salt of the earth type. I am. I am. Once you praise me, begin obeying me, you'll see. You'll see."

There was silence as the wind and rain reached a peak flurry. I stayed put, watching Dan from the higher table as he continued, speaking softly but clearly into the fire.

"Our construction industry and our energy policy is a joke. It sat- isfies me to say it's a joke, to see and to state that these leaders above me are really beneath me. I'm announcing I'm changing the policy." Dan's voice strengthened. "Only I have the mixture of intellect and hands-on experience to direct this country … in consideration of my barely sub-Olympic javelin skills, in consideration of my housing wealth entrenching me within the top fourteen-percent of wealth holders despite my relatively humble beginnings, in consideration of the excel- lent elasticity of Geraldine's ass, better than all my friends' women except for

Clements - but he's a terrible driver! I should like to thank the genetic reality of my parents for my combination of brain and brawn. I will articulate most effectively concepts in kilowatt usage to the gen- eral public. I can make systems work broadly, and create a better nation for all of us. I will enact all this by decree. Thank you; without the love of my family I wouldn't be the great man I am today."

I got up, slid the window open, stuck my head out and took in a long cool draught of air. The wind and rain had eased. I took the armchair opposite Dan – we had swapped spots from our initial seating.

"You're not empowered to enact anything, man," I told Dan with some urgency, feeling like a surrogate confessor.

"When it comes to furniture removal," Dan replied, "I see all the angles and utilize space superbly. I can see which load bearing wall needs … as with the excellent development of my chest … the stupidity of property developers, world leaders and tradesmen well beneath …"

I got up and scattered the fire; it was too early for it anyway. I went outside into the cool breeze and Dan followed me. He was in a daze. I stood by his car waiting for him, like waiting for a dog to understand, and finally Dan got into his driver's seat, his expression baffled, embarrassed like a drunk emerging from a disgrace. I told him to drive safely, and he was relieved at my warm handshake, and with the way I held his shoulder in my other hand as if to say it was nothing personal, that I realized he'd only spoken the way he had as he'd been animated by a force beyond both of us.

March 18 - We humans can now see the error that led us to believe in our superiority. Our creative hands and rapid mobility allow us to act swiftly on a thought and so shape reality with sudden strokes. Our achievements are wide and spectacular when compared to our be-rooted siblings who, in order to remain at one with mother earth, to be in per- petual empathy with her needs and tempo, have sacrificed the great gifts of moving about and doing a whole lot of stuff.

But as I walk through the forest, I become aware of my own freakishness. How is it possible to articulate this alien, woody gaze that has fallen upon me? It is the freakishness of a lifeform physically disconnected from the earth and moving not in it, but only over it. With the animals this capacity was odd, but not freakish, meaning it did not have an alarming aspect. Other animals did not have our overwhelming transformative power, the knowledge and know-how that destroys courtesy of the apple in Eden's garden. My hands, my feet, all my simple actions alarm me beneath this vegetable gaze.

Bit-by-bit, the fire hearth is overtaking the television set as my nightly companion. I hardly use my phone or laptop either. Cultural product oppresses me. Comedy shows are anxious with laughter need; drama is the feelings clashing machine depositing you at a fried chicken ad. The forest sways beyond indifferent, wordless and dignified. The forest whispers error, error, error.

I had a nightmare last night: On the fluttering forest leaves, I saw whirlwind images of people, like little holograms; famous people, ordinary people I know, have seen, and they were all doing their thing, all of them in their endless motions of work, leisure, and sustaining bio- logic functions.

Then all these people fluttering on the leaves stopped doing what they were doing and began eating their own hands down to the wrist and beyond until the little leaves, thousands of them, were little holographic pictures of human gore, and these leaves, which had become bits of flesh, fell off the trees onto the earth and decomposed into soil.

Dan … he … behaved like a confession. His brain is an endless competition. He's a nutcase! But he's also a decent, ordinary guy, which means .how many nutcases are out there? The forest out there, this sentience which knows without knowing, entered Dan's psyche through me. The vegetative kingdom, through Dan, revealed the egomania of our species. I must thank the profound forest for this truth.

I have half-a-dozen bottles of red wine from a discount supermarket in my kitchen. (They cost three dollars a bottle, but have always tasted good to me.) Tonight, me and the forest drink together – I'll pour one into the soil, in reverence, for every red I pour down my own gullet. Forest and I shall commune in the dark, under the moon - me and all my fern and eucalyptus friends. And I will invite forest deeper into my soul for even greater illuminations.

March 20 - Now I know. I think I know. Can it be that the passive is the most active? The vulnerable the most powerful? Is all that stuff in Christian mysticism true when they say the weak shall inherit the earth; and all that stuff in Taoism and Buddhism too about the yielding over- coming the hard, the soft overcoming the strong?

Can plants – can brainless nature - coordinate a response against us humans? It's not a new idea. Viruses, bacteria, these infinitesimal, mindless ones, can adapt to survive. In our bodies, when an infection invades, all manner of being, antibodies, fly into battle for us. We walk, chatter, flip through phones, munch on this or that, oblivious to the death struggle occurring right in the middle of our guts and pulsing through our blood. There are astonishing, invisible realms everywhere, but in this case, because of my humility, the greenly realm is giving me priv- ileged looks at its operation. So, it trusts me with its strategies. Why? What happened with Dan is just the tip of the iceberg.

This is the latest development:

Two nights ago, the arboreal kingdom and I drank well. Together, me, fern-tree and towering mountain ash gum, among others, went through the whole six bottles of plonk. You've never met such generous drinkers. The foreign, non-indigenous leafy ones, interlopers of the forest fringe who find a home here in the suburban yards which merge with the forest– sycamore, elm, birch, camellia and rhododendron tree– these refugees from all over the world – well, fern and gum did not want them to miss out, and so I poured libations for them, too. And who else needs a drink, the forest said, and I realized moon had been rudely left to sit on the edges of our carousing despite caressing all of us with its lights and shades and enlivening the whole evening with its feminine enigma. How can a man treat lovely moon with such shabbiness? I poured a libation to moon!

Then I went to bed, slept, and the force I can't name, that I have invited into my life, began its psychic germinations.

Moon glow entered laptop in my dark, curtained room. I saw my cousin Gilly on screen, on my short table at the foot of my futon. He was wearing a tank-top which showed off his lean, gym-built physique. It must have been late morning or early afternoon. He was in mid-con- versation ... with me. I was suffering on my mattress; I did not feel well; I was drooling, and there was a wide stain of crimson vomit over the edge of my bed and on the white carpet. I wondered what force had compelled Gilly to astral project across the city to me. I wanted water.

Gilligan is a successful financial securities analyst. He has a small segment on a news program reporting on economic issues. He was telling me about a business meeting and an after party where he seduced a young actress with a role in a police procedural. He seemed put out I'd never heard of her, or the show. He leant back in his chair and began stroking his torso under his tank-top with his long, fine fingers. My tongue came out in the motion of retching, but there was nothing in my stomach. I was wincing as Gilly relayed graphic, rapid informa- tion about his latest sexual conquest. His handsome face, mid-thirties, looked at least ten years younger. He insisted I pull the laptop onto my futon, close to my face.

"…superstar vagina," I heard him say.

"What? Superstar what?"

"Pity you don't watch crime shows. You see, once you've fucked a star, it's your cock that's in every show and that's what people are watching. I'm in culture, man. I am culture." He began explaining this theory to me, this transference of his libido into the public consciousness.

"Even if all that's true," I managed to grunt, "it's nothing to boast about. What about pornography," I reasoned, in a nightmare.

"How dare you try to belittle my victory," Gilly retorted in a high-pitched voice. "Go on, pull back your duvet, show me your stomach." He wouldn't shut up until I obeyed. He burst out laughing.

"No wonder you never get superstar vagina! This, this is how it's done." He pulled back from the camera, lifted up his tank top and pointed at his abdominal muscles. "This, with sit-ups holding ten kilo- gram weights behind my head, and all the while gauging commodity price movements pegged to the dollar; divination and muscle. You know the effects of government issuance of bonds to finance the deficit? I anticipate interest rate possibilities interfluxing . my word . with foreign exchange rate dynamics. Anticipate as I'm being fellated by superstar vagina, and yet you can't appreciate this, but you must, so here it is. I thank you for this interview; this following crescendo is your privilege and reward."

And then Gilly began singing. I didn't turn away, too captivated by the vulgarity of it all. He was singing an old number, a popular song from the eighties. No doubt he had formed an attachment to it from his earliest memories. His voice was not terrible, but flat and common. There was silence when he stopped. I was propped up on my elbow.

"So you're singing now," I said, trying to sound neutral, hearing the momentum of the wind heaving through the bristling forest, feeling something had been turned on that couldn't be turned off.

"Hear how graceful and heartfelt my singing is?" Gilly queried with enraptured confidence. "My singing evokes everything, completely, every color, from 1987. Maybe a few other people in the world can also do this, but they can hardly anticipate the price of zinc and offer cost-cutting supply chain options. They cannot seduce superstar vagina by pretending an interest in the star sign of Taurus whilst discussing open-plan living and over-capitalized assets."

"What is this about evocative singing, cousin?" I asked, fighting against the tide of his vanity and confidence. "Can you really believe you're a great singer? Can you even believe you're a good one? I won't rile you by saying your voice is atrocious – that's generally an overused assessment. What your voice is, like mine, is mediocre. Of course. You have no special talent for singing, like ninety-nine point nine percent of us. How could you have imagined otherwise?"

Gilly squinted. His mouth hung open like I'd slapped him. "I have no talent," he whispered to himself as if in a dream. I grew curious in the silence.

"How could you have imagined it?" I pressed him, seeing the wonder, the stirring wakefulness in his expression.

"I sing along to clips," he replied. "I've been academically gifted. I prepare excellent presentations and reports, and am photogenic. A pretty girl threw her arm around me once at Karaoke. Her hair fell down the side- of my neck. Fucked her that night … and almost her sister a few weeks later … fuck it! Can't believe I blew that … her fault! I've always considered myself a good mover in a disco. My dress sense is way better than average. I know more about debt to gross domestic product ratios and their meaning than … if you look at my shoes and compared them to yours, I mean your shoes, Nathan, your shoes …"

"But what does all that irrelevant crap mean?" I hissed. I got up and pulled back my curtains; I saw the roiling canopy in the grey gust. It was cold, and I was in my undies. "Jesus, Gilly," I said, returning to my futon, pulling my duvet back over me. "It's as if you've condensed all your perceived good qualities into a bottle, a tincture, some combustible element, and blown it up."

At that stage I saw my mother enter the screen on the left. "Your opinions about my singing have been noted and are now forbidden," Gilligan confided. "I'm thinking of being a gigolo. I've decided to pay you a small fee so you can promote me. There's nothing better happening in your life, anyway. Be ready for my instructions, and also …" Gilly was ordering, with a depraved half-smile, as I minimized and silenced him.

"Nathan," my mother said, her concerned expression filling half the screen, "I'm worried about you, son. Your life is all over the place. I blame that bitch, Karen. I know you think your life is your own, and I should mind my own business, but I really shouldn't. I created you in my body, and that makes me your creator, and so everything you do is a by-product of my initial creation, and so you are an extension only of me, like your sister, who refuses to be an endodontist even though I told her to be one, and to lose weight, particularly as her legs can get chunky and men don't like that. Men like firm calve muscles - studies have been done – and wearing high-heel shoes can develop them on your sister's legs – which are really my legs as I created them too – only mine were better in my prime … still not bad for my age … still not bad. I know you get angry at your mother for meddling, I know this, but that's only because you haven't acknowledged I created you and so own you. When you've cleaned someone's shit more than a thousand times, you have the right never to take them seriously again, never - this is the secret - and so I don't take your belief in your autonomy seriously - why would I? . Remember your nasty pimples and how I knew what to do? . You should not be allowed to make any decision without ."

And at that point I closed my laptop. Anything but to see a human face. Again, I got out of my warm bed, and I stuck my head out my window in the bracing autumn wind, drank the pure air so full of life and devoid of thought and everything became clearer. Better to lock myself in this cabin until my food ran out, and I dissolved stinking into the floorboards. The idea of human company sickened my heart.

But perhaps that was it. Was that the ultimate strategy? The forest wants life to survive the human cataclysm. Like its thirst for light, it thirsts for a new equilibrium. Through its vast powers of telepathy, a manifestation from the vege-monde, the Edenic stronghold, defends life against perilous humanity. The counter-attack has begun. It, this arboreal antidote, will do it through ego amplification - amplifying beyond all bounds the very thing threatening it with destruction. O forest genius! In the same way we drink its air in our physical symbiosis, we will drink in, unthinkingly, its subtle, psychic alterations.

It … I still don't have the right name for this psychic aspect of nature . will inflate our egos, making them massive and beyond regular narcissism as a galaxy is beyond a solar system. In the end … this would be it … anyone who won't idolize us, who won't take a lower position, will be our bitter enemy. We will not tolerate any contradiction. We will annihilate each other with our bare hands … or better yet . finding one another insufferable, non-validating, we will cut off communication and therefore all cooperation. No cooperation ... this will delete our human mobility, our action.

Yes ... we will remain alone in our small spaces, shunning com- pany, gratifying ourselves with second-hand life on televisions and computers, glutting ourselves on copied images as we shrivel and die alone. This entity wants to strand us first within the walls of our egos and then ... the four walls of our physical rooms. Then ... this had to be it, I understood ... the environment would regenerate, free of all that murderous human commerce and restlessness. Air would purify; emissions and heat wane.

O God! The diabolical beauty of it all! What kind of age are we entering? An age of the human ego exploding into supernova. Oh, this spiritual thing, primordial accelerant of vanity and pride, wants the end- game, wants to bring everything to a head in a sudden death struggle for planetary dominion. It's tired of our unholistic ignorance ... this ego inflating. monstrous . this Igor . this defender of nature . this gar- gantuan trickster of telepathy who makes us believe we can sing sweetly when our voices stink ... this ... Igorrius ... has come to bring forward a new day ... and ... Igorrius has proclaimed its herald. Me! But I don't want to be its herald! I don't want to stare into Eden's mirror at the ego-monstrosity of our self-knowing, apple-munching species.

Can it be that we have aimed to destroy nature not out of greed, but out of fear? Has the roaring wind frightened us so much that we decided to uproot the trees? To look out my window at night, with all the lights off, and to listen to the roar of the forest canopy is to know the earth mother, Gaia, exists to birth prodigies. Igorrius, new God, has catapulted from Gaia's uterus - that much is clear . but how to appease it? I must do something. Dinosaurs died under a new, post-meteor dawn as they were too big. Only the little things lived. There must be a way to make ourselves little again.

March Twenty-Something (Not sure as all communication devices have been off for days for self-defense purposes.)

Not wanting to see a human face, fearful of Igorrius' long reach, sensing that on the phone, on the news, whatever, I would be presented only with Igorrius' interpenetrative ability to catastrophically inflate egos to obscene, despicable proportions, I withdrew into the solitude.

Then today, like an animal sick with anxiety, whose fear of being exposed, of motion, suddenly flips to an understanding that remaining still is fatal, I counter-attacked my inertia, knowing my speculations could no longer remain to fester in the isolation that melts days into nights, knowing I must confront the unfiltered truth of the predicament, I went into the city today to confirm the universal influence of Igorrius.

It is confirmed. Never doubt the prodigious power of a new God mandated for action by Mother Nature. But still, the speed of it! Igorrius, in a few short days, has upended the world. Was this the first official day of his/her/its dominion? This is what I saw:

I entered the city on a near empty bus early afternoon; troubling augury. Very few people were in the city. How did it get so bad, so fast? Hypothesis – almost overnight, due to Igorrius's swift power, we have come to find one another .unendurable .foul.

Walking the ghostly city streets, it was clear to the sensitive eye that the people stood further from one another, suggestive of a heightened jealousy of space, of personal dominion. There were also many more mask wearers than usual. These were partial masks, over mouths and noses. Such people appeared like ancient, occult orders of silence who consider non-insiders stinking reprobates. (Note: new cults are consis- tent with apotheosis). Through this deployment of mask fashion, the new cult (exclusionary as cults will be) stated most eloquently – I have nothing to say to anybody, as my wisdom exceeds your understanding and my allegiances are fixed. The arrogance of it!

Alternate or parallel hypothesis (even more calamitous): the mask wearers are so deluded, they believe themselves celebrities and are jealous of hiding their identity, fearful of fantasized paparazzi and autograph hunters, their ego controls fully blown in convictions of baseless fame.

And that's just the people on the streets. Of those already self-captured within the four walls of not only their mental but physical space, no speculation can be too outrageous. They are perhaps already dead. Autophagy - self-cannibalism - can be hypothesized.

I approached three sets of strangers to inquire why the city was so silenced, but they looked at me with apprehension, fearfully, like I was a ghost from another age, Pre-Igorrius. One man scampered away without a word. Among the quick utterances the others gave before they also moved on, I heard repeated what sounded like the word "crown". So Igorrius is already recognized as the king of this world? Can the coronation precede the herald? The gods work too fast!

I left the limbo city; one not quite dead but not alive either.

0 ADI (Anno Domini Igorrius) Day 5 (or perhaps four. Unlikely to be three - have been meditating/contemplating/creating a lot with doors locked, curtains drawn shut, devices off.)

To have all the lights out in the house and to see – to sense and hear – the power of the forest roaring in the bracing wind beneath the soft chords of moonlight is to know beauty and menace and to under- stand we humans are less significant than we think and we forget this at our peril.

Nightly, with all my devices off, Igorrius reached me through the pure medium of the small fire in my living room, which instructed me with its glowing hymn of warmth and obliteration, with its non-human movie, non-human album, which sang and narrated a story of the cycles of form and energy, sacrifice and re-birth. With the raw, clean instincts of a Neanderthal I understood my lessons. I knew what I had to do, so I took my drastic step.

The dire purgatorial ritual is complete. I have lit the fire in the forest, the terrifying fire, the destruction that must precede the creation, tabula rasa, blank slate, based on me tearing humanity to shreds in cut- ting flames. All is obliterated and all, I hope, shall renew out of this human compost of stricken ash. Tomorrow, I shall reconnect with the world through my various instruments to see its condition, and the con- sequences of my act. I can only hope the Age of Igorius is a brief one, and that we may soon emerge into a new dawn, a neo-Eden, with our leafy co-earthlings. Nothing is certain.

The following is a confession of my annihilating act against the human virus. This is what I have done:

Firstly, I drew pictures of people doing stuff. All sorts of stuff we think is great that plants can't do. I'm an average drawer, but it's the intention that counts when you come before a god. I drew people running, people playing pianos, people fixing windows. I looked into mag- azines lying around the cabin for ideas and drew people looking down microscopes, people holding phones, fixing boats, drew people exam- ining fossils . but why continue? People doing, doing and doing. I did a picture of a man walking on the moon (I made his face especially impudent and domineering, as best I could). I drew nearly a hundred of these pictures - filled an exercise book.

Then, collecting my incendiary devices, I walked past my old com- panions, ferns A and B, and bowed deeply. Then I bowed deeply to the gum trees, the other ferns, and all the introduced plants too like the rho- dodendrons - I bowed to camellia and agapanthus, bowed to the weeds. I bowed to my co-animals of the air and the earth who, despite their mobility, do not profane. Then I began the purgatorial inflammation with these words:

"O Igorrius! - Dread Igorrius! - born vengefully from Eden's defiled womb – forgive us this species that worships itself in its vulgar, self-re- flecting idolatry!"

The day was soft and blue with a gentle breeze. I fluttered the pages of my exercise book into the breeze so that the god would see the nature of my offering. Then I put the book into a metal buck. I tipped lighter fluid on it, adding the following words:

"All human activity is nothing without you, Igorrius! It is born in symbiosis with you and, unharnessed to you, is sacrilege. I confine all these activities to ashes - to be compost to the mighty forest - as we humans must be in the end, no matter how great we think we are. May we never forget that we owe our animation to you!"

And then I set the fire!

And it burned and burned in my little bucket, all that human action eaten by the flames, eaten right up, and it felt great, great, to see it all blacken like that. Then I got the hose and put water in the bucket until it was all black swill, and I found the tallest mountain ash tree in the yard, a monster of a guy, perhaps a hundred-meters high, and I poured out the swill at the base of its trunk.

Then I sat down, reclined on a bit of grass with my hands locked behind my head and looked up at that tree. I felt good; calmer than ever. A hundred meters tall! I began wondering how old that particular tree was, what it had lived through. I wondered why it liked it up here, in these hills in particular. I'll have to look it up; I'm as ignorant as; I have a lot to learn. And while I was pondering that tree, a cockatoo on one of its highest branches let off an insane shriek. God it was funny, how a mad creature like that also wanted to have its say. But then, all will be well with the little cockatoo because its crazy little soul is allied with the forest and the forest, I'm confident of it, is forgiving that way.

Glenn Cannon is a Melbourne, Australia, based writer and casual teacher. After receiving a BA in Economics from the University of Melbourne he worked odd jobs, returning to the same university years later to complete a Graduate Diploma in Arts (Literature). He subsequently lived and worked in Japan, where he contributed short fiction to micro presses before authoring two novellas, titled, respectively, *Hicky Knocky* and *Forsaken Blossoms*. These works have received positive independent reviews that can be found on the web or on his website: www.gallery350ppm.com/past-publications.html

ELIZABETH GENOVISE

Meridian

The funerals are long over and I'm told that Norman Hall has been scrubbed thoroughly enough for the bleach to mask the lingering smell of copper. The building is still closed, its shredded walls awaiting their butterfly keys, but the prayer vigils and candlelit circles have dissipated; there are no more gaggles of hand-holding girls and hoodie-cloaked boys circling the flower-studded crosses stabbed into the lawn. We are a shocking statistic—nineteen dead, including the shooter—and yet we are already old news. Like the reporters, the faculty and students seem to be willing to leave it at that, in the interest of returning to the business of living. But I am caught in a vortex that won't let me go, and I have been here before.

Of course it would happen to Eva, I overheard a colleague say in the parking lot one morning. *Of course it would be her classroom. That's God for you, after the hell she went through the year before last.*

I'd spoken to Sean Wakefield exactly once. He was listed as one of my advisees the year before his killing spree and he came to see me sometime in August. He slumped in my extra chair and described in monotone his plan to take the easiest teachers and then "get the fuck out." I was tired of similar routines from idiot children who didn't know why they were in college, and I lacked the energy to ask him questions about his long-term plans. I gave him the information he needed to register for the fall semester and told him to email me if he had problems. Then I went back to tapping away at my keyboard, and at first I didn't notice that he lingered there in the doorway, arms crossed. When at last I looked up, I said curtly, "Was there something else?", and he shook his head and slunk away. I didn't look into his eyes again until the first week of December when he chose my classroom door, like a game show player selecting his prize, and walked in with one handgun held high and the other holstered at his hip. There was no warning; mine was the first of three classrooms he would enter that day before the police swarmed him and he stuck the gun in his own mouth. My students screamed and clamored toward the back wall, but Sean was unfazed, training his focus entirely on me for the space of ten seconds. I think my hands were up, but I can't be sure. I only know that neither of us spoke a word before his gaze dismissed me and he turned and open-fired on my students. My memory after that is of blood and tissue slung along the walls and across the oatmeal-colored tile. It's of clawing fingers and jerking limbs and blurred faces mouthing words I couldn't understand, and then of my own hands fumbling to pressurize a wound only to be instantly soaked with red heat.

Hours later, when the ambulances were packed and the campus secured, a paramedic said to me, "It's all over now; try not to relive it in your head."

It was exactly what a counselor had told me two years earlier when a woman in a Lexus forced my husband and five-year-old daughter off the interstate and down a fifty-foot embankment, where Clyde's skull broke apart and Alyce's body was mangled beyond recognition. *It's all over now.* Only it wasn't, it never is. I am reliving it all over again. I am traveling two parallel roads, rocking back and forth to keep balance, even when I know they end in the same place.

It's different each time I re-imagine it. I rarely sleep, and these visions come to me in the heat of day, as vivid and bone-shaking as life. I am lucid. I am fully in control. In one version, I have a gun of my own concealed in my leather satchel. When Sean Wakefield enters my classroom, I am quick and decisive: I draw the weapon out of the leather folds before he can meet my eyes. I spin toward him, and fire once straight into his chest. The sound is shattering. Sean goes down hard, rocking the floor, and blood spools out from his jacket in the shape of an S. I have protected my students, but I am no guardian angel in this fantasy. I am Death, and I am both frigid and smoldering, glorying in my victory as I stand over his twisted body. When I snap out of it, there is always a dizzying moment in which I expect to be back in my home, with the smell of Clyde's aftershave floating through the hall, or the sound of Alyce's plastic pony galloping down the banister. But of course these things are now ghosts; I am in a third-floor apartment with a sterile kitchen and a living room furnished with ruins. The clock above my kitchen table stopped working months ago and I've never bothered to fix it, preferring the morbidity of that silence.

Back before I lost my husband and daughter, I understood why ancient peoples so rarely returned to their cities after the raids and the fires. I thought, how could people live among the charred pillars and the cracked bowls without losing their minds? Yet here I am thriving in rooms like tombs. I've discovered that I am not of those docile tribes who wished only for clay walls and freshwater springs, the comfort of corn and mortar and pestle. I am of the warrior class, carrying the fury of defeat with me like an axe slung over my shoulder, and I am waiting my chance to surprise the old city and hack down its usurpers in the night.

They have pushed my history classes into the science building, Hughes Hall, and I have no choice but to share a classroom wall with a young physics adjunct named Ira Layne. His voice is warm but loud, his passion palpable through the drywall, and he has a bad habit of taking his analogies too far. The silver static on your TV, he tells his students one Monday, is left over from the Big Bang—microwaves that are literally the afterglow of the universe's beginning. "Think of that screen, and now think what happens when you change the channel, to images of human faces," he says, pounding something—probably the whiteboard—for emphasis. "It's an analogy for what we've done, for the miraculous nature of what we've become, since that total chaos. The seed of it all was a moment of pure violence."

And then, later in the week: "It's like yin and yang, guys. White shot through with black, black pinpointed by light. You can't have life without that duality, without the collision. It's the oldest truth we know."

I've seen him in the faculty breakroom in Hughes. He scribbles in a notebook, and from where I sit, it looks like poetry, but I don't care enough to ask. Ira sits in his corner eating peanut butter sandwiches, and when he's not scribbling his verse, he's like everyone else on this campus: watching me as though I might detonate at any time.

Just about everyone save Ira knows what happened to my family, about this time two years ago. The newspapers and internet saw to that. What they don't know is that a few months after the woman—her name is not a name worth saying—evaded responsibility with the help of a high-priced lawyer, I hired a P.I. to follow her. The P.I. was a graduate student at another university forty minutes away, paying his way through a Ph.D. by tracking down people's wayward lovers and screwup children, and when we met to discuss the terms, he looked bored until I told him my story. Suddenly his black eyes sparked to life. I saw in his face that there was some personal grievance of his own at work here, that he wanted to take this woman down almost as much as I did, and I didn't ask why. It didn't take much imagination really. She very likely represented all that he hated in the world; she was wealthy and spoiled and above the law, and probably racist, too.

I knew it without ever having seen her in person. "You almost sound like what you need is an assassin, not a P.I.," Robert said at one point, a small smile playing at the corner of his mouth. I sipped my ice water. I almost smiled back.

"Watch her," I said. "I want to know everything."

I have searched Ira's face for a similar small smile, for the glint in the eye that means he knows, has seen how ugly it all is. But his face is moonlike, just a shining blank, and his lectures persist in their passion.

"The universe's deepest secrets are in the void," Ira tells his students one Wednesday, his voice practically rattling our shared wall. "As far back as Aristotle, we've worried about what was out there in the ether. He was the one who said, 'Nature abhors a vacuum,' and that was the commonly-held belief for a very long time, and for good reason. It wasn't just that people were afraid of the idea of nothingness. If you think about it, it was also just common sense. Consider what happens when you suck soda out of a straw. . . "

I tune out the rest, garnering energy for a lecture of my own. We're talking about early Communism in Russia, and I know how this will play out. "Yes, the long-term consequences were ugly, but understand their reasoning," I say, tapping my marker against my palm. "They wanted a level playing field. They were tired of the one percent. Is that so different than now? In a society where men oppress women, where the wealthy crush the poor, where even the best attempts at equity fail because the old systems are so entrenched? In a place where 'justice' belongs to whoever's got the big-ticket lawyer?"

Five minutes later, I have what I want: they're arguing amongst themselves, and all I have to do is sit back and watch. There it is—the glint, the cynical smile. It's always this way, the smallest seed branching out into a thousand arguments, a thousand resentments rising from beneath old logs like worms after a hard rain.

In another reimagining, I have a knife. It's the kind of knife I've seen in the movies—huge, a glittering crescent moon. When Sean steps into the room, I whip the blade from its black sheath and in a single swift motion slice it through his abdomen. He makes a sound somewhere between a scream and a sob and then slips in his own viscera, careening sideways into the wall. The gore is horrifying and beautiful at once, the livid colors a match for what seethes inside my own body. Sean spasms on the floor, sliding around in the red, and his eyes shift back and forth in a frantic nystagmus, unable to focus. Their power is gone. I step back from the mess and calmly lead my students out of the room. I don't look back.

I overhear Ira talking with another adjunct about his apartment. It's a studio, and he's sleeping on the floor, saving up for a real mattress. He's good-natured about it but he paints a dreary picture. I want to tell him what Robert, my P.I., reported to me about ten days after our first meeting. The woman who murdered my family was forty-six years old and a college graduate, but had stopped working at the age of thirty, when she inherited several million dollars from her father. How Robert uncovered all this, I never knew. "This house she's living in—it's big, but it looks like it was built in a day," Robert asked, leaning forward over his beer. "It's falling apart, built on an anthill. Up on this mountain above Maryville. Just one person living there like an animal."

"What do you mean, like an animal?"

He'd been watching her closely, taking chances I'd not expected him to take. He described the way she dressed—like a bedraggled czar or deposed queen, odd capes and hats and big jewelry—and told me how rarely she left the house. One afternoon, he followed her down the Maryville post office where he got close enough to smell her ("foul," he said, "like she hadn't bathed in weeks"); and here, she elbowed her way to the front of a long line and told the postmaster she needed to be served first.

"She has someone making her a custom dollhouse," Robert reported. "And dolls to match her and her dogs. She was sending him pictures and instructions. She literally stood there and told all this to the postal guy with all these people waiting behind her staring at her like *what the fuck?"*

I wrote him the first of many checks. I had already sold the house I'd lived in with Clyde and Alyce, unable to pay the mortgage without Clyde's income; what did I need with money now anyway? I told him to keep at it and to meet me in a week. In case there was any chance of him falling off the wagon, forgetting me in the urgency of his graduate work, I showed him a photograph of Alyce when she was four.

"Closed casket," I said before tucking the photograph in his jacket pocket. "Remember that."

If only I could tell all this to Ira, who has found a way to make even the void romantic.

"A bell inside the void is silent," he tells his students, "but create a void in a glass box, and you can still see the bell standing inside it. That means something is conducting the light. Which means out there in space, in what we called the void, there is something conducting wavelengths of light. And so there is, in fact, no such thing as *nothing*. The collisions are happening everywhere. There are endless battles of matter and anti-matter, all the time, virtual particles popping in and out of existence. What some physicists think is that at the beginning, positive matter found like matter, and managed to link up into a kind of wavelength runway."

My own students are listening, heads cocked. Even when I say, "This next set of questions will definitely show up on the exam," they don't blink. I curse Ira's booming voice, his impossible zeal.

"We understood nothing, not even about electrons shuffling around in the atom, until we understood the void," Ira says. "Nothing."

She had help, Robert told me a few weeks into his investigation. She was able-bodied, but she had a fleet of young people who came to the house every day to care for the lawn, the pets, the laundry, the trash, everything. He watched them move in and out of the house and eventually found a way to speak to one of them off the property.

"What she wants," he told me as he handed me a pen for his check, "is not just people doing her chores. I think she wants people to worship her. She likes the power she has over them. She pays them exorbitant rates to do her shit work, and they get stuck, and they're afraid to leave, and she loves it."

"How do you know all this?"

"The one I talked to—I told him I was looking for work. He's twenty-five, Eva. Twenty-five and he can't tear himself away. He says it's the easiest money he's ever made, and that as long as he treats her like a queen, she'll never fire him." His eyes were shooting fire again. "Hispanic kid," he went on after a pause. "Smart, too, I could tell. And he's going to be there God knows how long, cleaning her slop, flattering her to get his wages. She pays them to affirm her in her disgusting self-adoration, is what she does."

I waited a beat. "What's your degree in again, Robert?"

"I've told you, psychology."

"Apparently you're in the right field." It was hard to keep my face neutral; no profession disgusted me more after my experience with grief counselors. "What else did you find?"

"I followed her into a bookstore in town, this place that's apparently in danger of closing. She offered the owner money to bail him out, but said she had to be in control of the stock. The owner wasn't having it." He sat back. "Specifically, she wanted to do away with the religious section. All of it—Christianity, Buddhism, Taoism, every book on the shelf."

"And this offends you?"

His head snapped up. "Of course. It doesn't offend you?"

I handed him his check.

There once was a God in my life, a myth my parents drew in the air. The more I saw of the world, the harder it became to make out the contours of this vague figure, and when I began to study history, I understood that gods had been our own invention and always would be. It didn't matter what part of the world or what culture from which they'd sprung; they were all flaccid, helpless to exercise justice despite the wondrous qualities their human makers had assigned them. Only the Greeks earned my respect with their slutty, self-obsessed divinities. They didn't bother to idealize. Their gods were just men and women endowed with the power we've always wanted for ourselves, and they dealt out death and judgment as they saw fit, not in accordance with any ersatz morality. They never turned the other cheek, as no sane human would.

Ira has the gall to sit beside me at one of the round tables in the breakroom. "I've heard that my classes are disrupting yours," he says, biting his lower lip. He looks so young, in that particular way people empty of experience look young. I can just picture him proudly turning the other cheek, and then standing there stunned when he got hit.

He's wearing his usual high-necked button-down shirt with the sleeves rolled up around his elbows, the way my husband used to wear his, and the watch on his left wrist could be the same watch I bought Clyde on his thirtieth birthday. It was a kingly gift, as I was living on adjunct pay in those days. Back then, I found nothing sexier than a rolled-up shirtsleeve paired with a heavy wristwatch, but on Ira it's ridiculous, the props of a child playing dress-up. His arms are hairless, too pale. His skin and body remind me of the play-food Alyce used to keep in a plastic refrigerator, each glossy piece frozen in perpetual freshness. I think, he has never suffered so much as a headache in his starry little life.

He bumbles on: "It's Eva, right? I'm sorry-I'm just part-time here. Really hoping that will change soon, though. They gave me three classes, which is pretty good for a first-semester adjunct." He tries to smile. I'm not helping him. "Anyway—I'll try to quiet down a little. I didn't realize how far my voice carries. One of your students mentioned it to me."

"Let me get this straight. This is your first semester. So you applied to work here *after* what happened? After the shooting."

A pause. "Yes. Just after Christmas."

"I believe that's what our psychology professors would call *death drive*," I say dryly. "Do you know how many people quit, how many students pulled out, after last November? This is the worst enrollment we've ever had."

"Yes." He fidgets, and I realize he's got that old notebook curled over in his lap. "Would you believe me if I said I came here because of what happened?"

I just stare at him.

"That didn't come out right. It's hard to explain. It's just—if anything like that happens again, I mean to be ready. To protect these kids." He's fumbling, beginning to color up. "Not that I'm any hero. Just the opposite. But sometimes I envy people who have the chance to jump in front of a train for somebody else. You know what I'm talking about? At least, the ones who take it." And I realize I've been wrong—he hasn't been waiting for me to detonate, because he doesn't know. He's an adjunct who speaks to no one, and he doesn't know it was my classroom that was ravaged first last fall.

"Wait til it happens," I say, pushing back from the table. "This rescue scenario of yours won't be so romantic." Then, before he can respond, "Just try to tone it down in your eleven o'clock. My students can't focus with you booming on the other side of the wall."

"You got it." He unpacks his lunch—a peanut butter sandwich on cheap white bread. It's ascetic and spare, a monk's lunch. There's an awkward pause, inside of which it occurs to me that he means to stay right here and eat with me. He's waiting for me to unpack my own food.

"I have a meeting," I say, rising with my lunchbag in hand.

"Oh. Sorry to keep you. I hope it goes well." His eyes, hazel in the sun filtering through the breakroom's solitary window, meet mine. Their color is a match for Alyce's. In the space of three seconds, he looks at me as though he'd like to pull open my drawers and closet doors and dig around in the contents. Then he looks away, pulls a book out of his backpack so that he can read while he finishes his pitiful sandwich.

I turn quickly away, my heels clicking hard against the tile floor as I exit the room. What I'm thinking about is this: Robert claimed the woman rarely left her house after dark, save for Friday nights, when she returned to the bookstore she'd tried to buy out. She went alone, bought herself a fat brownie from the mini-café, and then sat there gorging herself while reading before she returned home. Once a week. Once a week, alone, after dark, at a bookstore on the outskirts of town. These four facts became a mantra that played over and over in my head for weeks as I worked and showered and lay awake through the nights.

Sometimes, I don't have a gun or knife, but I anticipate Sean's coming and I bolt the door. My students stare in bafflement as I snap the lock into place and then drag over the heavy lectern, which I wedge just beneath the handle. Next I overturn a metal folding table and slide it in front of the lectern. When Sean tries the door handle, I begin to laugh. I can hear him cursing and grunting there on the other side of the wood. He fires a few rounds into the door but they lodge somewhere in the lectern and go no further. I am still laughing, laughing as he curses me. Once more, I am no guardian. The victory does not lie in my students' safety. It is in his enraged cries, and in my elated escape from those cold and probing eyes. He will not look at me today. He will not fire that gaze into my flesh and make me doubt.

"There are rumors," my dean says to me in a private meeting in March. "Your classes are divisive, Eva. That's the word I'm hearing."

"Divisive," I repeat, blank.

"This isn't the first time I've heard it, either. I don't understand how it happens, what you're doing in there." She's a frosty blonde, perfectly made-up, and she's the type of woman who's used to getting what she wants simply because she's beautiful. Men and women alike have been falling over themselves to please her since she was twelve. Her blue eyes narrow as she considers me in my rumpled dress. "I understand all you've been through," she continues. "But really, Eva. You put me in a difficult position. Considering what this college has been through this year, you'd think your focus would be on bringing these students together, not the reverse."

"My students are ignorant," I say. "If my classes are divisive, it's of their own making." And I mean it. They're spoiled and empty-headed, these kids, with their intact families and easy part-time jobs and unscarred pasts. The ones from the city think they're urbane and interesting when really they're just walking I-Phones. The ones from the country only speak Baptist and stare blankly when they hear a word outside the vocabulary. I can size up any one of them in ten seconds or less.

My dean says, "There must be something in the way you're presenting the material."

When I don't answer, her icy gaze shifts to her computer. One pink manicured nail taps the mouse to awaken the screen. "It's world history, Eva. Introduction to world history. Just teach the timelines. Can you do that?"

While we're on the topic of teaching the bare facts, I'd like to mention Ira's hammy lectures, but she's not his boss, and it's clear she's finished with me anyway. I nod at her profile and calmly show myself out. Nothing about her comments has surprised me; I'm certain that she knows nothing of history at all, short of her own.

When I do sleep these days, my dreams are Ira's electrons—a handful of particles trapped in a tiny vessel where they ricochet off the walls and crash into one another with nowhere else to go. When I'm not reliving those horrific few minutes with Sean Wakefield, I am dreaming the same triad of dreams, over and over. In the first, I am lying on my stomach in a patch of black, piney woods, balancing a shotgun against a rock. In the open field beyond the tree line are wolves-four or five of them gathered in a gash of moonlight, licking and ripping at the body of a buck who is not quite dead, his back hooves pawing hopelessly at the grass as tendons tear and bones snap. I sight the biggest of the wolves through the scope of the shotgun. My finger finds the trigger, carbon-dark and slick with sweat. The wolf's head lifts from the deer's guts and the moonlight is blue metal in the animal's eyes. I can see the reams of blood between long, white teeth. I fire; the wolf collapses atop the mauled deer and the rest of the pack scatters. I walk into the field's sudden silence and then I shoot the deer dead before I drag the wolf's corpse into wakefulness.

The second dream is a surrealist painter's fantasy, Mary Shelley's wet dream. I am in a dark workshop knitting together silver-furred bits of wolf into a kind of doll—a pup with a pointed little face and per- fect nose. It's a gift for Alyce, but it's not coming together right; my hands are shaking and the stitches are crooked. The creature purrs to life when I attach the tail and then it takes its first wobbly steps across the worktable's surface. One leg is inches too short. One pointed velvet ear is turned backward. The tiny wolf falls in a heap and makes a pitiful mewling sound. I think, *I cannot give this to Alyce. It's too terrible.* But I can't kill it either, this innocent creature with its tinsel fur standing on end and baffled eyes searching mine for an explanation.

The third dream is actually a memory. Clyde and I are on our first real vacation together, before Alyce's birth, and we're driving down a lonely, ice-edged highway in Colorado. The Rockies on either side blush coral as the sun falls. We haven't seen a town or another car in an hour. Then something quivers into view up ahead, wraithlike and silver in the snow. It's standing in the dead center of the road. Clyde applies the brakes, murmuring a question. We come to a complete stop. It is a wolf standing there, perfectly erect and unafraid, his blue-green gaze locked on us. He doesn't move. We don't move. Clyde reaches out to stop the windshield wipers' dance, as if afraid to break some delicate commu- nion with the animal. The wolf watches us a moment longer and then trots left over the heap of snow curdled at the roadside and into a stand of green-black pines, where he vanishes.

Sometimes the order of the dreams varies. I see the mountain wolf, I kill it in the fields, I stitch it back to life. I sew the wolf together, I see it on the road, I shoot it from the woods. Each sequence is as terrible and right as the other. I don't ask myself what it means. These are not physics I want to understand.

An innocent like Ira only knows the world's better half—people who do their jobs and take care of their families and believe in common decency as a rule. People like my husband or daughter, to whom the impulse to wound would never occur. I never saw their killer's house with my own eyes, but still, I know it, and I wish I could walk Ira through it and watch as his moon-eyes went wide.

About a year ago, three months into our partnership, Robert broke into that house. Or rather, he walked through a half-open back door on one of her bookstore nights. Over an untouched cup of coffee he told me he had never been so disturbed. "The animals—even with the servants there, she can't keep after them," he said. "There was dog shit everywhere, wedged up against the furniture, and the whole place smelled like cat urine. Everything was filthy. The kitchen-rotting food on dishes stacked up everywhere, silverware all over the place. The win- dows so cloudy you couldn't see out of them. There were pills every- where. She must be on nine different medications." A pause. "I don't know what kind of scum she's got for a psychiatrist, or if she's playing two or three of them to get what she wants, but nobody should be on that many medications."

I sipped my iced tea and said, "Did you look at the bottles to see what they were?"

"Xanax. Prozac. Ambien. Klonopin. Other benzodiazepines. She's the kind of person who would literally die without her pills. It would be like heroin withdrawal, times ten."

I straightened up in my chair. I saw myself overturning the orange bottles into her toilet and flushing . . . then her, spasming on the floor in the agonies of withdrawal. Of course, she would only call her doc- tors and ask for more. Pain was not the province of such people; it was entirely reserved for the decent.

Robert said something else, and I started. "What?"

"I said, the real crime here is the doctor who's destroying her mind with this shit." His mouth was a hard line. "The profession is rank with this."

"And you'll be different," I said.

"Are you patronizing me?"

"No. It's just—well, young graduate students. It doesn't matter the field. You all think you're going to change the fucking world. And in a few years, you'll see it doesn't make a damn difference what you do."

He studied me a long moment until I looked away. Then, his tone leveling, he said, "You know, you're a cold fish. I never met a woman like you, and that's no compliment." When I didn't respond, he rose and slid his chair back in. "I understand that you've been through hell. I understand what you want. But this woman—she's just a sick person, a zero. She was probably doped up on those pills when she drove them off the road. But you've got murder in your eyes. I wonder if you even know it."

"So did you, Gandhi, not so long ago," I retorted. "It's been there since you started watching her, since you figured out what she was."

"I know it has. The difference is, I'm not going to let this go any further than a feeling. I'm not going to let it rot me from the inside. You—I wouldn't be surprised to see you on the news one night." Seeing me reach for my purse, he added, "I think this would be a good time to end this. Let's call this my last paycheck. I'm sorry."

I nodded. I signed the check, held it out to him, and turned to leave.

On a Sunday night I fall asleep, or into a kind of trance, before my computer. In my half-dream I am crouched in the bushes outside Sean Wakefield's house, waiting for dawn, waiting for him to emerge from his ramshackle duplex with his weapons. I have a hunter's net stretched between my hands. I will snare him, then beat him with a Louisville slugger once he's down, and I will start with the face, the eyes . . . I can hear him moving in the house. I'm poised to leap. Then I hear something overhead but far away, like the crinkling of tissue paper, and look up to find the sky shockingly bright with stars. There are billions of them, their light reaching the earth in a way Ira once told his class never could be possible due to the universe's eternal expansion. The crinkling noise becomes the words *luminiferous aether* and in my trance I remember what they mean: the void that isn't really a void. The so-called vacuum that bears witness to infinite collisions, the most radiant deaths and survivals. I see pictures in the constellations: human faces, landscapes, and finally, the outline of a wolf. So absorbed am I in this strange vision that I don't hear Sean exit the house or even start his car. I forget the net and the baseball bat waiting in the shrubs. I forget even my fury, and then I am awake.

    I feel cheated, enraged at myself for my weakness, even if it was only a dream. I would not have dreamed such a thing a year ago. Back then, after Robert quit me, I purchased a small knife at a pawn shop and began carrying it with me everywhere. It was not the kind of knife you'd see in the movies. It was slender and practical, but it would suffice. At any given time, it was in my purse or my right pocket. I practiced removing it swiftly and without fuss. I imagined how quickly it might sink into a soft belly or an exposed back. I'd be out of the alley and into my car within minutes. On the way home, in the dark, I'd throw the blade into the Clinch River. She would bleed out in the dirt, where those like her had forever belonged. It was the sort of justice that demanded too much effort from most gods, who were afraid to draw the line.

It is with just such a little knife that I stop Sean Wakefield in another of my fantasies. The vision comes to me in mid-April, on a sunny afternoon as I sit alone in my office with the door closed. He has just arrived on campus and I am running late preparing for class. I hear his sluggish footsteps in the hallway and I know. The knife is in my hand. Just as he passes, I throw open my door and lunge; the blade is true, sinking into his spine, and I drive it in a second time as he falls to his knees. His back is to me. The gun falls out of his hands and clatters across the hallway floor. His body seizes twice and I'm certain he's dead. Then, the fantasy becomes nightmare: he slowly turns his head, and I see silver fur instead of skin. His ears are pointed velvet. When his eyes find mine, they are the warm hazel of Ira's eyes, of Alyce's eyes, and I stagger back against the wall and scream.

In the two years since that woman murdered my family, I have tried to make a ladder of my anger, as an ancient climber faced with a rock wall would make ropes of whatever fibrous life lay at hand. There is no scaling a loss like this save with the hardiest of tools. There is no time for memories or tears. At night I sit in Clyde's old chair, and I sleep on Alyce's old pillowcases, but I do not let myself remember anything beyond my anger. I can't afford to.

Then Ira stops me in the library one Thursday to look at a photograph in a glossy hardback. "It's a picture, the best we have, of the Big Bang—how the light and energy spread out after," he says, pointing. He's got some peanut butter from lunch smeared in the corner of his mouth. "Can you even believe we have a thing like this?" At first it just looks like Earth, but stretched. It's a long oval shot through with red, yellow, and green pixels of light, the colors jumbled and battling one another, spread thin in some places and gathered hotly together in others. I remember how my husband, a brilliant man, had a strange childlike love for weather radar, taking immense delight in pictures that looked just like this one. "You see that? *That's* a storm," he'd say, pointing to a colored mass moving in from the west. He'd be joyful, even a little smug, as though he'd concocted the thunder just to please me.

Shakily I say to Ira, "I could be looking at anything."

"But you aren't."

His head is bent as he studies the photograph. It's bent at such an angle that I can see down the neck of his high-collared shirt, and I start a little, unsure. Hideous raised scars mangle the skin there and vanish down his back. I imagine what could have happened to him: Struck by lightning? Some heinous abuse at the hands of a father? Shrapnel? He is old enough to have served in the military and come back. I heard something awhile back about a new faculty member who'd finished school on GI money. But the scars could be a year old, or ten. I remember what he said about jumping in front of a train, and before I can stop myself, I say, "What happened, Ira? What are you doing at this school the semester after a shooting?"

He straightens up, closes the book. He looks at me with those pale green eyes as if trying to decide whether he should respond. "I was a coward, and I got away with it," he says finally. "That's all there is to it, all that's worth saying. I hope I never get away with it again."

"You're crazy," I mutter.

"Probably. But maybe it takes one to know one." A pause; an attempt at a smile. "Good thing we're in different departments, huh? Or you'd blackball me for tenure for saying that."

I hurry back to my office and lock the door behind me.

Maybe it takes one to know one. But Ira couldn't know me if he tried, and if I told him how far I went last year, how close I came to being the precise opposite of this dreamy hero he hopes to be, he would know not to sit with me at lunch tables or show me pictures in his books.

I didn't dare show my face at that bookstore on the outskirts of Maryville more than once, and so I chose my Friday with care. It was the first week of December. I sat a few tables away in the grimy little cafe as she gorged herself on chocolate and bent her head over a book whose title I couldn't read. She wore a heavy maroon cape over an ill-fitting skirt and blouse. She did not tip the young waitress. When she wanted a coffee refill, she snapped her fingers in the air to get the girl's attention. She read her book, and every so often, she would startle me with a laugh—a disturbing laugh, forced and breathless. It was obvious she wanted someone to notice her and ask what was so clever in her book, but the other patrons rolled their eyes, as though they'd seen this before. At one point she reached down under the belt of her skirt and seemed to grope or pick at herself. I could smell her. *A sick person, a zero,* Robert had told me, but sickness was not a pass. I imagined her that day on the highway, speeding fifteen over the limit, losing control of the Lexus and ramming my husband's Honda from behind. I could see Clyde frantically overcompensating, his right hand instinctively flying out to protect me even though I wasn't in the car; it was what he always did if he had to stop suddenly for a red light. I could hear him calling Alyce's name as she screamed in the backseat. *It's all right, hang on, baby* and then his voice would be lost in the explosion of gas and glass.

This woman . . . she kept on driving. She was smart enough to call her lawyer before she called 911, but she kept on driving.

I watched her until she left, and then I got up and followed her into the December air. I glimpsed the book's cover—it was something about dollhouses, and I remembered Robert's report. She'd ordered a dollhouse and a set of dolls to look like her and her dogs. The blood was singing in my ears as she walked around the back of the store and started down the narrow alley that was now dark. On the opposite end was the gravel lot where Robert had told me she always parked her car. I fell into step behind her, the knife in my sweatshirt pocket. When she paused to check something in her purse, I stopped, too; when she resumed her unsteady walk, I did the same. She moved incredibly slowly and yet somehow I failed to make my move.

We were almost to the end of the alley. All was silent. It would be easy make a quick leap forward, grab her filthy arm with one hand as I drove the knife in with the other. But suddenly all I could think of was what would happen after. Somehow, I'd be caught. Somewhere, there'd be a hidden camera. There'd be a trial and then jail, a lifetime in a concrete box while she recovered in a ritzy hospital and then treated herself to a six-month spa stay somewhere in Europe to reward herself for having pulled through her little trauma. Always, her kind would win. Always, evil triumphed, and good men and sweet little girls fell through fire and rotted in graves. I couldn't bear to give her one more victim- me. This wasn't a matter of guilt or morality staying my hand. It was the last card I held, the only victory available to me, and playing it birthed a new, deeper fury that would be as raw the day Sean Wakefield entered my classroom as it was there in the alley.

As if to affirm my choice, a pair of shadows flitted across the light at the end of the alley, and a teenaged couple started toward us with their arms slung around each other. I dropped the knife and walked away.

Ira checks the glossy book out of the library and slips it under my office door the final week of class. I don't know what he expects me to do with it, until I notice the bit of loose-leaf serving as a bookmark on page 41. It's not the photograph he showed me before, but something else: a computer-generated image of a glass box, inside which two particles are suspended in air, confronting each other like warriors. One black, one white. Arrows point down to a sequence of images, like a flip-book in slow motion, in which the particles meet, cancel each other out, and then pop back into the box. There is no written explanation on this page, but it doesn't matter; I remember Ira's lecture. At the beginning of time, light found light. I see it as my daughter's wooden Brio tracks, slowly dovetailing together to form a superhighway for existence. Impossible. Pure theory. And yet here in my memory is Alyce's sturdy little locomotive trailing passenger cars and a red caboose, chugging across the living room floor on some errand of life.

Maybe he's known all along whose classroom Sean Wakefield picked first.

I mean to return the book to the library before I leave campus, but for some reason it stays in my lap all the way home. Back in my apartment, I sit down at the kitchen table and close my eyes. Sean is right there, standing in my classroom, gun held high. That horrible gaze meets mine for the space of ten seconds. For the first time, I speak to him: *Why? Why are you looking at me?* His answer is only that gaze, which lingers on and on, long past the moment where in real life he turned aside from me and fired upon my students. He stares, and I am stripped to my bones. I know he sees everything—the murderer in me, the spirit of Cain and Judas that entered me when my husband and child were killed. The hatred I'd festered for so many people who had ceased to be people at all and had become only ideas. I hated counselors, doctors, lawyers. I hated complacent students, a whole generation of ignorant teenagers. I hated both the wealthy and the unemployed. I hated happy families, intact families. I hated the beautiful and the innocent and the naïve. I hated believers. I spent my days teaching my students to look at the world as a sphere divided into two halves, the black and the white, the evil and the good, when all along, always, I knew that the meridian was indelibly inside each one of us.

In waking life, Sean Wakefield looked into my eyes and saw that I was not worth killing because, like him, I had already been extinguished. He'd never once sat in my class, but it takes one to know one. I was a living justification for what he was about to do.

Now, in this vision, I hold out my left hand. *Wait. Please.* Slowly, so he can see it, I draw the knife out of my purse with my right hand. Sean's eyes follow my hand. I can see his puzzlement, the question coming to him. Still in slow motion I open the blade and hold its tip to my left palm, where my second and third finger meet. I cut into my own skin and draw the knife down in a straight line. The blood blooms out of the wound. I meet Sean's gaze. *I am no different. I am no better.*

Take me, not them.

His face relaxes. He turns the gun away from my students, and onto me. He fires, and I wake to the sound of my kitchen clock ticking.

The morning after this final vision, I am too tired to think. I drive through the city on autopilot, then surprise myself by pulling into a deli a few blocks from campus. I order a thick roast-beef sandwich wrapped in foil along with a bright yellow apple and a bottle of mineral water. I remember the adjunct diet and how peanut butter and cheap carbohydrates used to sour my stomach. In the breakroom I use a black Expo marker to write *IRA* on the white deli bag, then stick it in the fridge where he usually puts his sorry lunch. It is stupid; it is nothing. But I have been away for so long that I don't know where else to start.

I teach my classes. I hold my office hours. I go home.

Alone in my apartment, I sit in the dark and switch on the television. The first screen is one of silver static, the crackling aftermath of the universe's beginning. My eyes water from the effort of separating the pixels from their counterparts. It is a hopeless task, and the darkness around me deepens the longer I sit gazing into this violence. My head begins to pound. When at last I lift the remote and change the channel, human faces appear on screen, and the whole room shifts, refracting a light I am not quite ready to see.

Elizabeth Genovise has been an O. Henry Prize recipient, a multiple Pushcart nominee, and an inductee into the Tennessee Literary Hall of Fame. Her short stories have appeared in many literary journals, and her third collection of stories, *Posing Nude for the Saints*, was published by Texas Review Press in 2019. She carries an MFA in fiction from McNeese State University in Louisiana and currently lives in east Tennessee.

ANDREW REICHARD

Titanomachy

You've heard it said that every story has been told. Also: everything is meaningless. Of course, but that's not a cause for despair, nor need it be heeded, because when the Teacher says "everything" he must be speaking as a poet.

Very far away from most places, an Empire collapsed on a planet called Kath, or sometimes called Kronos by those attuned to the repetition inherent in the story. The Empire, colonizer (or castrator, depending on the teller) of the sky (or Uranus, if you like) turned in the end on its own children until it had nothing further to consume, so it consumed itself. Many people told and foretold this story even during this great destructive harvest of what was once a great nation. Many people tell the story now, light-eons away, shaking their heads at one or another star they believe to be related to Kath, or close enough: waving at the northeastern quadrant of the sky will do, if you happen to figure on the southern hemisphere of such-and-such a planet. But some understand that it will happen again, and again after that, perhaps even here...

~

In a storm-riddled but benign day in the pang season-the first of Oktoyear—an older but not yet elderly man closed a book and rubbed his eyes.

He knew he had understood the words he'd read, perhaps had retained their meaning in some narthex of his mind, but he couldn't bear a single idea to focus now. Ceasing to rub his eyes, he took up the occupation of looking out the window. Old and almost bare trees bent their branches in the wind. Wet clumps of leaves adhered to the equipment across the yard and then, in a shift of air, tore away like bandages or scabs, leaving the unblemished metallic surfaces beneath.

He was watching the girl in the weather-breaker for a little while before he knew his focus wasn't on the weather itself. She among the domes and antennae, moving from panel to panel, reaching up in knuckle gloves and instructing some adjustment to laser-bright buttons before clapping the lid closed, trudging to the next figure. A saucer-shaped satellite might have tilted one fraction of an inch at her command. But it might have been the wind. These long Patmos pang-days, subsisting on coffee that somehow tasted wet, if that made any sense, and equally wet cragoat's cheese. There was only ever one taste in his mouth. But, here at the end of all things, who was he to complain of the food?

The comm-pickup he'd left by the stove chirped. He could see her talking to her wrist: <*Zzzzhhh*—these are about done. *Ssssshh*—to look at the emer receptor, and then I'll be in.>

"Mind you don't track mud into the bay," he said from his stance by the window.

In the field, she looked up toward his outlook and waved. No rude gestures or "cheek" from Sedeq. She wasn't meek, nor did she maintain any particular posture toward an old man out of formality or what his long late wife would have called "etiquette." She was simply very nice. Incurably cheery—the more so, it seemed, in proportion to his petulance; which sometimes was, he would admit to himself, a flourish simply to marvel at the resulting affability of this young and gifted colleague.

If she hadn't the anchorite's disposition he had come to expect;—if she claimed not to mind the coffee, the weather, the impenetrable quiet of the planet, this old man's company, if she went energetically to her day's tasks—whether trudging among the hardware in the moor or sifting her large eyes through the datastreams that looked to him like emissions of digital smog—then she claimed so and did so in perfect candor. She'd done it for long enough in his presence that he no longer subscribed to his certainty that it was an act. He'd put it out of his mind. It was easier to be taken by her smile and her bright, alto "good mornings," than to persist in the apprehension that Sedeq was simply an outstanding actor and as dispirited as he.

He might never know the truth. On this byway of a godforsaken planet, no one stayed long except he. To the next scientific charter that came along, Sedeq would probably leave him, though warmly embraced he would have been in her parting. And after that, he'd be able to, now and again, when the sentiment took him, glance up at the night and mutter "that ship's ascended" before letting his eyes fall back to one of these books, these tomes, these volumes, many of them barely any better than novels for all the *information* they offered.

~

The principle of the story is that it's been told before. By the Ancient (relatively speaking) Greeks, the Romans, the Mayans. They use calendars, oracles, dreams, dice: any object or state of mind to which signs and portents adhere like wet leaves to upheaval, and after the story is told, in its simplest form, then in its wake come the poets and bards: to count the syllables and arrange the sounds of bedlam, the slouching towards Bethlehem.

The principle of these stories is to bring us low, to situate us back on the ground from which our minds have flown like golden gods. That is their worth and their labor, which, when complete, remain as objects, not readily cautionary as they generally spare nothing, repeated and empty and eager to point out all kinds of repetitions that might be patterns or simple conformities to the arrangements of existence and unexistence, but they are always understood to be stories, and that is their limit no matter how often reiterated.

In someplace other than here, there was war in the sky, in a place, a planet, with a name, or in the heavens at large, powers, pantheons, were rising or falling, and it was certain to everyone involved (in some corner of their minds) that the rising powers would fall and the falling powers would be dashed to pieces on the rocks; which, in the end, might signify, these rocks, for the stories that would one day be told about them.

~

"You know, I'll go blind before I find an iota of real material on our subject," he complained to her that evening over canned soup, which she hadn't let him eat straight from the can (simply because she preferred porcelain, and it wasn't any trouble to take down a second bowl).

Sedeq was so sure he was joking that maybe he was. She chuckled, visibly looking for the right words to tell the joke: how silly he was being, worrying for his eyes "when if even the stars were—"

"Going out," he interrupted, waving at her with his spoon.

"And when they're all out, we'll all be blind," she said, sample of something they often said to each other genially enough on cloudy nights when they couldn't otherwise be watching the stars.

Condescendingly, lovingly, he told her not to be dramatic; even if they lost a star every minute from now on (and that didn't seem likely!), she and her children would be long passed before the sky out here was noticeably dimmer at night. "On Earth, they'd never even have noticed—"

"I probably won't have children, I've decided."

He looked at her because of something in her voice he guessed hadn't been intentional, though he wasn't sure what it was.

"I'm not being dramatic." Sedeq moved aside the empty cans and sat on the counter, hoisted herself up easily, her ankles crossed and her feet made shapeless by thick wool socks. "It's more that I'm being overly calm, calculated, maybe: because it's just that I don't care to explain to any child why her mama's fixated on the blank spots in the sky. I'd have to join the ranks of those new astronomers who position the telescope carefully and say, 'Now look, that's where a star used to be. See it? That space where we used to see a little dot of light: we call what used to be there Kronos now, or Elyôn, though it used to only have a number assigned to it, so unimportant and far away was it, until it vanished, suddenly. Or, see that little area in the deep zone beyond the Butterfly Galaxy? There're so many *other* stars there that you wouldn't know anything was absent unless you happen to study absence, but now we call that Salpizo-7, the star that's gone, because now we only have names for the stars that are no longer—" she jumped down from the counter, her feet thumping the floor, though she walked lightly around the room, the table where he was eating. "So, you see, it's actually that I'm completely undramatic; it's just that there are conversations I don't care to have with a child who wouldn't even understand when they were older, and probably—because these things are so small and far away—care. And I wouldn't be able to make them care if they didn't, even if I tried to explain to them what these conversations meant."

"But you care," he said, still seated, eating, listening. He was afraid she would say, or give some indication of thinking, *enough to be stuck here on this rock with you*. He wanted to offer her a chance to make that clear: that she was not happy here, despite what she showed.

She said, "It's important work. I care."

"Someone has to do it," he said.

But for some people that was enough justification for any number of things, and Sedeq was, "Dauntless," he said, shaking his old head in admiration and enough maudlin wag of jowl so that she beamed at him in answer.

They often said that their work was 'undramatic.' While other scientific eyes watched the bright auras of supernovas, Sedeq spent all her time in matching past starcharts with the heavens as they currently looked to find the missing pieces. Even with the assistance of IGSA databases, this was tedious work. Undramatic, but not trivial. And they weren't always immune to melodrama.

"Have you ever wondered about that prophesy from the Book of Revelation in the Bible? About a third of the stars going dark?" she asked on a clear, windy night while they lay wrapped in their bedrolls on the hill in the lee of a satellite disk. Though she'd brought with it the caveat that it might have been some stellar dust obscuring her view, she had found what she thought was another one: *unfound* neither of them were ever able not to say, as if the universe were playing some trite linguistic joke. She'd taken him out of his studies in the dead of night to not see it.

"Of course I have," he said. "That's why this station is called Patmos. We're all dreaming God's dream and all of that sort of rhetoric. But you're a scientist." He looked up into the heavens, as the ancients had called the space, and saw a lot of stars obscured by his own cold breath. "My great, great, great, *great* grandfather was a Baptist," she said. "Had some kind of specific ideas about that book, I understand, from an old pamphlet he published. This is hearsay; I never read it."

"Have to go back that far to find some Christianity in your line, eh?"
"Not at all. After his generation, we reformed and became Catholics."

"You're very dear to me, Sedeq," he said. "I understand that you must move on from here soon, that this must feel like exile for you, and I would never wish that you stay longer than you had to; but, nonetheless, I have—I've enjoyed your company."

"You're not as much of a grump as you think you are," she said, he thought, fondly. She was smiling. Though he was not looking at her and wouldn't, now that his vision had stirred into one great milk-swill of stars and tears, Sedeq sounded like she was smiling and like she knew he was a sentimental old thing who was losing his grip out here on an ellipsoidal and moonless planet so far from anything else that it was not good for much else but sidereal research.

~

"And the fourth angel sounded, and the third part of the sun was smitten, and the third part of the moon, and the third part of the stars; so as the third part of them was darkened [1]*"*

~

---

1. Revelation 8:12a

Of Patmos, he might have said that night came often and almost instantaneously, but never lasted long.

Most of the trees had not much more upward growth than what brought the tallest to twice his own height, still accounting for his stoop. He'd once shared space with a biologist, who'd worked for roughly a month before colliding with a lethargic depression and retreating to the cyro bed for the remainder of his term. The geologist that had swapped places with the biologist only made it three weeks and was still sleeping since no one had remembered to wake the poor man for the charter that had brought Sedeq. He felt very bad about this.

But not being the type of thinker whose happiness depended on the diversity of life, he'd taught himself to love, if not the homogeneity, then call it the oneness of Patmos the planet—the congruity, the simplicity of its short and unimpressive food chain and weather-battered sameness of year-long seasons that, on walks like this, entered his consciousness as of a dream: the faded edges, the mind's limited capacity for details when its focus remained fixed on a broader narrative of absences making space in the sky.

He had learned to love its ugliness and would go walking in the bounce-step of just under a g, never roaming far from the outpost—sometimes not farther than to crest the line of hills that passed for mountains here and to marvel luminously along the star-chart of his life, unable to see it (his life) as anything more definite or dimensional than a chart.

Very quickly, it seemed to him, the mind arrived at a kind of tipping point between space and time. As space (so too light and matter) lessened, time thus increased its pace to fill the void, like a molecule ricocheting more and more quickly from contracting walls. The walls, of course, represented death. Death as walls and floor and ceiling without a door through which to escape. When the capsule that was death had drawn inward enough so that it matched, roughly, the dimensions of his self, then the dream would end, and the death-room would be a coffin instead of a room.

Until then, time would put on more and more speed; and this sense of terrible swiftness toward terrible darkness, even while the velocity of the doings (generally speaking) of his life had run almost to a halt, was somehow intensified by the knowledge of the disappearing of stars across the known universe.

Each star was, in and of itself, quite meaningless, of course. But sometimes he felt he couldn't do without a single one, and that each star gone missing—vaporized, perhaps, by the sheer will of the one repeated story—each of those stars, now absent forever, had come to seem like the Source of knowledge, as if knowledge was jumping from sinking ship to sinking ship, staying a single pair of quarks away from full nothingness.

Or perhaps it was all already a black hole and all knowledge had already been consumed and they were already in the dark. Yes, this seemed more reasonable. There had to be a spiritual reason for the existence of so much darkness. Not a very scientific thought, but neither were the majority of his thoughts.

"Alluring devils, black holes," he'd said to her one evening. Or perhaps he'd used the word *tempting*: "Tempting devils, black holes," and it had been morning instead of evening, Patmos turning toward their star to the northeast. A very old and red star, theirs. Its light often brought to his mind only a single word: *senescence*.

"If it doesn't vanish on us, like I've just confirmed with Near Base that Sy-N10 apparently has, it'll go supernova in only a few billion years, probably," said Sedeq from the far side of her computers. A pale blue light was on her lips, but her voice was as lively as ever, singing over the rattle of the furnace. "But with stars, there's always safety in numbers!"

"Ah—we call that a numerical preponderance," he grumbled for the sake of remaining in character.

She would spend an entire four-hour day among the emer receptor lines, pen between her teeth or sometimes humming very beautifully, reporting and verifying her unfindings with other outposts across this system and the next, stopping only when the senescent star of Patmos would have screened her signals; and then she would emerge from around the deck of screens and stretch and go for her weather-breaker and dross boots and slip outside, stepping quietly so as not to disturb him in his reading.

Though he knew it well, he still often returned to the Bible, to the book of Revelation, which he understood, theologically, to be a message primarily not of despair, though it seemed so clouded in so many numbers. He supposed that he was almost as sick of numbers as he was of words.

Hoping that Sedeq was listening on the comm (though, he didn't address her) he said aloud from his desk, "If God wanted we not meddle in the spirituality of mathematical quantities, why would he then have assigned a number to the beast of John's dream?" Not looking for an answer, not wishing for one, simply wishing that she would know what was in his mind. These words he had rehearsed in his head before speaking aloud, and, by then, he'd already for- gotten what they meant. But how precise and rhythmic he'd made them sound! Pronouncing 'mathematical' with all of its five syllables, as was proper.

She had work to do and no time to heed an old man's half-serious obsession with signs and theories and how to put them, though he reserved the right to entertain and announce all manner of thoughts, sensical and not.

Though she'd been too busy to answer while out working, at the table that evening she drew on a napkin a diagram of the sun, one-third of it dark. She used a highlighter for the two-thirds that would still be hot and bright and a black marker for the part that would no longer be, and she spent a minute or two being careful to keep her markings inside the lines.

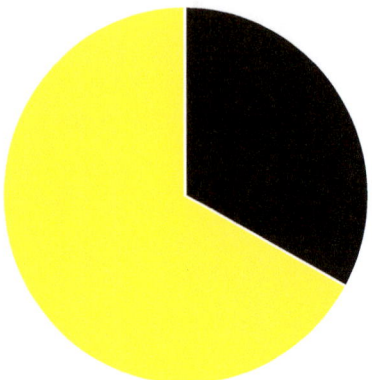

"You're very good at drawing circles," he said, taking the finished work in his hands and rubbing his thumb over the sun.

"Of course, it probably wouldn't be like a pie-graph third smitten, with radii from the center—who knows—but, in two-dimensions, it's just easier to find the coordinates for the center and then from there."

~

...luminous blue variables, maybe, but there's still a lot we don't know about those, and, in the past, they've been recorded—like with the one in PHL 293B galaxy—as having shone brightly beforehand, before disappearing, which these don't, these stars. These are simply—we simply wake, or settle down in front of the telescope one night to find them missing. And the only reason we even know they're missing is because—well, a few, like frickin', like Omega Piscium were obvious, even to some casual stargazers, but most of them we only know are missing because we're using loads of mapping and actually looking for the missing stars, and there might be thousands or...millions of missing stars we just haven't noticed yet...and, sure, there've probably been stars

disappearing this way for ages, no one the wiser, and there have been a few, what are sometimes called "massive fails" recorded throughout the 21st century, so, yea, with that many stars...but what we're seeing now, we're seeing this happening all the time. Just about every day some binocular-toting novice on a cattle ranch on Earth...we don't want to commit any errors in logic here, or cause any undue excitement, but, from where we stand, it does seem like...well the rate at which we're unseeing stars is...is incredible, really...

~

"and the day shone not for a third part of it, and the night likewise." [2]

~

In an effort to record an approximation of the basic narrative he figured himself, and everyone, to be living—and somehow feeling that he should position his narrative in the past tense (which, chiefly, was what required it to be written down)—he wrote with a blue-inked pen on a blank sheet of graph paper,

The stars were going out

That seemed a good enough linguistic application of the problem at hand. But from that point, an almost infinite number of directions presented themselves. For instance, he could (and probably should) temper the drastic-sounding nature of the statement above with a condition, something like,

but not too many of them (stars, that is)

But, even laying aside the horrendously awkward word order and, come to think of it, redundancy (he could polish that later), he realized that he'd have to further condition the condition to add weight back in the former direction—something to the effect of,

that they knew of, yet

And then, rapidly,

---

2. Revelation 8:12b

> *but they were finding more all the time*

And because the turn of phrase had become automatic, he added,

> *or unfinding, as the case may be*

Then, just before he lost his patience and crumpled the graph paper savagely, the incomplete thought,

> *though, this was not necessarily a cause for*

~

This allows the Teacher to say, with conviction, something like "Everything is meaningless"—because, when we see through the drama of the despair at hand, we are given to understand the subtext of this blanket statement, which might be expressed as: "except, of course, for one or two things."

But only a statement that encompasses, engulfs, everything can attain perfection. We can't settle for anything less than everything because, in this sort of philosophical (or religious) mode, we feel that either everything is meaningless or nothing is meaningless; and how are we to decide, then, which of these is the more terrifying?

Thus, we have the wise and measured statement: Everything is meaningless. Kol hebel, *to transliterate the Hebrew, assuming that's useful to you. Then, later on in the text, "there is nothing new under the sun"* ('ayin l)adas tal)at semes). *Both of which statements become a kind of mantra that create what is popularly called a "self-fulfilling prophecy." Because these two statements—"everything is meaningless" and "there is nothing new under the sun"—engulf everything (including nothing), they not only grasp hold of whatever we might want to consider new or meaningful and effectively ban it from the meaning of the words "new" and "meaningful" (including the words themselves, creating a structure of complete meaninglessness), they also—and this is very important—become a kind of shorthand for what we might call a* total belief.

The fact that these statements of the Teacher do not lead to an equally total despair *by those who have canonized this text into their system of beliefs (but, in fact, lead to the opposite!) means either that the words and their import are not taken seriously, or else that there is, as understood by the conscientious believer, something situated outside the dominion of Everything, beyond the monarchy of the word Meaning, or the word New, or the suffix 'ness'-indeed, beyond and above what can be contained within the functions of language and thought—that Something which the ancient Hebrews called YHWH—which word is only a kind of half-word or half-name, a mere breath, because they also understood that to name something was to attempt to enfold it into the realm of thought, of humanness, which had, in fact, not yet hap—*

~

She had been sitting for a long time in thought at the table with a cold cup of coffee between her hands. The hood of her sweatshirt had caught the coarse bun she'd tied loosely up and had stayed there, giving her head an enlarged look. Motionless, as she so rarely was, he at his desk began to worry. But he couldn't think of anything to say to break the silence except to read to her passages of what he had in front of him, which he didn't want to do. He sat considering other topics of talk: the time, the weather, the stars, their stock of supplies. Working together in such a small and secluded habitat, they had from each other just enough personal space for the important privacies, but little beyond that. She knew of his medicine cabinet, which he'd never tried to keep hidden, and had undoubtedly heard him straining from time to time in some pain and had never commented, even with her eyes. His eyes had fallen now and again on her tube of anti-fungal cream or her underwear, but never lingered. They would obligingly bundle each other's laundry from washing machine to drying without a second thought or complaint, sometimes even fold it. They'd learned a kind of familial rest around each other that embodied their bodies, which they kept as comfortable as they could, comforted too (he was, at least) by the other's presence: her unconscious tapping while at work, of no discernable rhythm, the undaunted concentration in her eyes and how she sometimes rode the office chair across the workspace with a single and accurate push to something she needed over there, her black hair and skin dark among the eggshell objects around them—her face and hands; she liked her wool socks, but sometimes a swatch of side or stomach when she stood and stretched. His tone was paler and pallorous. Stooped and sluggish. When cleaning, he always seemed to see more of his own grey hairs lying around, though he had fewer and they were shorter. When thinking, his hands burrowed into his outer clothing and clenched, while hers formulated a series of expanding shapes that often culminated in her pointing at the sky.

"Should I be worried?" he said finally. His voice seemed to surprise her. How rarely she rubbed her eyes as she was doing now. He hadn't noticed before.

"Worried about what?"

"I've never noticed you to sit still for so long." Might he have sounded paternal, and did he have the right?

He imagined she might have pulled her knees up to sit cozily cross-legged in the straight-backed chair, which she'd never, to his knowledge, done and didn't now.

"I'm just thinking—this is my job, and yet I still keep having to remind my mind that these stars we're unseeing, that they're, many of them, billions of lightyears away."

He was somehow saddened by the fact that she was working, struck by a working-thought. He'd been longing to tell her—with great self-lessness and consideration—to go forth from here so that she no long need be sad, take the next shuttle to somewhere else, and don't forget poor old frozen Hobbs, the geologist! and live her life, with children or without, and maybe remember him from time to time, if she wished.

He said, "So the information of their light going out is coming to us billions of years later than the actual event."

"Exactly, and my first inclination is always to let this calm me down 'cause, after all, it happened so long ago, and everything is so, so vast…"

"But…" He was often struck by how she didn't seem, to him, sad. He was confounded, frustrated by this.

"Well but that's just how small my own mind is, that I have to keep reminding myself—"

"Your mind is not small, Sedeq—"

"Because then I'm reminded that, while some stars are billions of lightyears away, others are, like, billions of *parsecs* out there, and others are much closer—only one or two hundred thousand lightyears away."

"Practically speaking, next door neighbors."

"As far as the universe is concerned, yea. So with all the massive variation in distance between these stars, I just thought—and, you know, I've thought of this before, but sometimes it just hits you—is how is it that all of these disappearances seem to us to be happening very close together on the timeline of events—and I mean basically on the scale of a fraction of a nanosecond apart, all of them, all at these massively varied distances. It's really—" and her hands were tangled in her hair.

He bumped the open book on his desk half an inch away from him. Then he shifted it a quarter inch back.

"What I wonder, what I think this means is that either our information, our entire structure of thinking about this, is meaningless; or else the answer to the question of why these stars are disappearing…to that Answer, things like space and time are, meaningless." She didn't really sound sure about that last word, but she said it.

"Are we talking about God?"

"If not him, we're talking about something new, something—well, sure, yea, we're talking about him."

"You're a Catholic, and I'm…" He touched his own hair.

She laughed. "What are you?"

"Some kind of mystic, I think. A hermit. Protegee of John the dreamer."

"You're grandiloquent, is what you are."

"And very very maudlin."

"Why don't you leave here?"

He might have turned to look out the window at 'here', but somehow couldn't make his brain tell his muscles to contort in that manner, so he smiled instead. "I came here because I left some other place. If I go somewhere else, it will only be a matter of time before someone asks me that same question."

Now, she had pulled her knees up to sit cozily cross-legged in the straight-backed chair, and he was somehow relieved by this.

"I had a thought earlier that made me laugh because I thought it sounded like something you would think."

"What thought?" He was eager to know, though he wondered if she was just trying to cheer him up.

"Well, I asked myself if this, these stars disappearing were a cause of fear to me, personally. You know, like existentially." She erased everything with her hands, laughing. "I don't know what kind of fear, exactly—"

"Small-time fear. Day-to-day fear."

"Sure! Blue-collar fear. Petty-theft fear."

"That kind of fear."

"Exactly…so I asked myself if I felt this fear, re: a lot of stars vanishing. And then I thought: No, I guess not, not really, but *it is exciting to get terrified about cosmic events!*" Her laughter rose an octave, and she almost looked embarrassed.

He was delighted by this phrase, cupping his hands together, holding them out to her. He had been reading Daniel—the book of Daniel from the Bible—and he almost slapped his hand down on the desk and said that he hoped—no, not hoped, *believed*, he almost said—that there was a place where people, good and righteous people, like Sedeq, shone like the stars forever and ever. In fact, he only just restrained himself from saying this, managing to make himself turn back to his books instead and duck his head demurely.

~

The principle of the story is that it's been told before. Every story under every sun and even, or especially, the story of the end. Very far away from most places, but also here too, there was a Country, a Kingdom, an Empire, a titan with a name and a harvest-shaped blade or a sword that sought some dominance before it ate itself (or imploded, if you like) in a great cataclysm that became an old story. The possible reasons for this destruction are manifold, but the result was never in question, even from the beginning. In many places, all at once, stars were dying in great multitudes, without a sound or a brightness, and this was distressing to those who were watching (though it made those bloodthirsty poets gleeful!) because it meant something different to each of them as it still seemed some way off, and there might still be time, at the very least, for another story, the telling of which would prove that it hadn't happened, not quite yet—

~

Now that it had come time for her to leave Patmos, he wished for her to remember him: even in ten, twenty years to think about him occasionally. She said she'd send him messages, of course, that they'd keep in touch, and in her tone he heard, implicit, the proof of her understanding that he had needed her and had been carried along by her presence.

He tried not to say anything maudlin. The charter was still a month distant, and then it was only a day or two out—four-hour days, at that. He tried not to say anything maudlin. They talked about the stars.

"You know, it's so easy to talk about super novas, black holes, stars vanishing: these are just words. It's even easy to begin to contemplate (though, we can't, really) the level of destruction that words like those represent, assuming this isn't happening near any inhabited worlds…"

"But you should try to make them understand," he said.

"Who?"

"The children."

Her look might have been stern. "The children I'm not having."

"Well, if you ever change your mind. But it doesn't have to be your own children. Let them at least hear about the stars, and they can decide for themselves if they care or not. I think that, at least, is important."

"Someone has to do it," she said, smiling at him.

Sedeq was leaving because "they're transferring me," but he knew that she herself had sought out the new position; she couldn't stay any longer on empty Patmos, to which they'd turned their thoughts and talk —Patmos in the pang-season, as he'd so called it, having put quite a number of names to its aspects, seasons, even some of the trees, to make it seem to them, not more real, but more graspable: this little ellipsoid world that was always hazy at the edges, rimed with a blue haze like the sort he associated with dreams: a fume of low cloud, a dimness.

"Someday, they'll build a city here," he said, his hands clenched inside his coat pockets. "Or a ring of smaller settlements—something like that."

"You'll be its founder," Sedeq said encouragingly. But she still had some work to do, much of it outside among the items of equipment that to him were little more than monuments.

He couldn't see himself from her perspective: his appearance when she looked up at the tall moor-facing window and waved to him from her work among the monuments. She always took the time to do this and then, when she came in, to try to convince him to "transfer" too. But, though they had this argument many times over the course of the wait, he never would relent. His place was here, he would say, finally, thinking: Some might say that since the story of the end has been told, the end has already happened. But, most likely, even the end only travels at the speed of light. Or, if faster, perhaps only a little faster.

Now, there is nothing to do but wait. Well, that, and—how was he to put it to himself?-waiting demanded a proper posture. He'd decide on the right words later.

END

Andrew is an author who lives in Grand Rapids, Michigan. His short fiction has appeared in journals such as *The Collagist*, *Black Static*, *Into the Void*, *decomP*, and others. His story "A Prayer" appeared in Volume One of this journal.

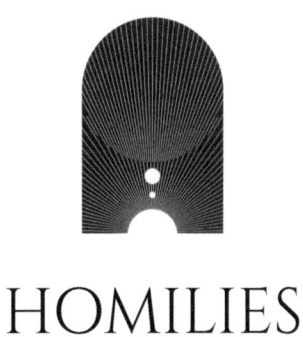

HOMILIES

RYAN DIAZ

The Holy Present

I. A Disclaimer

The preacher finds himself in a precarious position when he is tasked to preach on anxiety. The preacher is keenly aware of his inadequacy and shortcomings. He knows he is neither a psychologist nor a psychiatrist. He is a preacher, a pastor, one charged with the care of souls, and while he trembles at his post, he is also sure of his conviction that the scriptures speak to the anxious hearts hidden within his pews.

So today, I will not try to be a psychologist. I will not attempt to minimize the contributions made by those in psychology by generalizing and over-spiritualizing what is, for many, an important and pressing issue. I will, however, not speak around the issue. Though I may not be able to speak to the mental processes that produce anxiety nor write a prescription to combat them, I can speak to the state of our souls in which fear finds its birth and takes its root. The delineation between body and soul is a modern invention and inconsistent with the worldview of scripture. As St. Aquinas says, we are ensouled bodies and embodied souls, and indeed the state of one affects the other. So I encourage you, find a counselor, someone qualified to treat the mind but do not dismiss the humble preacher before you, for he has been entrusted with the care of your soul.

II. What is anxiety?

To face a thing, one must do the hard work of naming a thing, exposing it for what it is. Only then can it be met with sword drawn and slain. Yet, a clinical definition of anxiety will not do; we all know what concern is in a clinical sense. We can identify it as one recognizes the symptoms of a cold. The question is, can we name it? That feeling, that overwhelming dread of the future that sends us running into our foxholes or worse, pursuing the vices we'd once sworn to give up. We need more than a cold string of psychological jargon, and we need more than a mere textbook description. For us to unmask anxiety and face it, we must first turn to the poets. George MacDonald, the Scottish preacher, and storyteller called anxiety, "The care that is filling your mind at this moment, or but waiting till you lay the book aside to leap upon you-that need which is no need, is a demon sucking at the spring of your life." We all know this feeling far too well; it is that gnawing sensation, the clawing at the back of our brains that demand we give it our attention less all our future spirals into chaos. Anxiety is the desperate need to be in control, the need to master time and fate. It is a demon sucking at the spring of our lives, demanding more and more from us, robbing us of life, till we are mere shells of ourselves, human faces hiding a whirlwind of worry.

We have named it, but now we must face it, and to face it, we must get to the root of it. This will require us to answer two key questions: how did that life-sucking demon get there in the first place, and how do we finally slay the beast and find true freedom.

III. Matthew 6:25-34

Jesus' audience had every reason to be anxious. The ancient Roman world was not a comfortable place to live. Every day was a fight for life as 1st century Jews navigated the treacherous waters of Roman over-taxation and military occupation. It is to these people Jesus said, "Do not worry about your life." The audacity, to tell a predominately impoverished population, that their chief concern should not be the very things they needed to survive. Yet, a closer look at Jesus's words reveals that he is not callously calling people to forget their troubles. He is instead calling them to take on a radically new perspective.

It is curious to note that Jesus's words on worry come right after discussing wealth and its power over us. Before his appeal, "Do not worry about your life," Jesus warns, "You cannot serve God and money." Jesus understood that the dangers of money do not just lie in the greed it produces. Money is a means of control. By accumulating it and using it, we believe the false notion that we can control our lives, that we can be "masters of our fates and captains of our souls." It's this belief that changes our relationship with God and creation. If we genuinely believe we can control our lives, we no longer need a caring creator, and we fall for the false hope that we can exercise our will over the created order. The great irony is that by trying to control our world, we instead lose control. We are burdened by cares meant for a creator and not a creature. Anxiety stems from a desire to control our lives. It denies God his rightful place as creator by placing control in our hands.

In turn, we become less than human; rather than coming fully alive in the creator's freedom, we are enslaved to our cares. Life is more than what we eat, drink, or wear. Being human is not about controlling every aspect of our lives but instead giving up control and resting in the Sabbath rest of God, knowing that he will care for us. But we give up that rest when we supplant God. When we give in to the Serpent's lie and try to be like God, try to be more than human, we ironically become less human, less fulfilled, a shell of worry and anxieties, children trying to control the tides ignorant of the moon's pull.

We are deluded into believing we can control the future and determine the outcomes of our lives. But this is a fool's game, "The next hour, the next moment, is as much beyond our grasp and as much in God's care as that a hundred years away. Care for the next minute is just as foolish as care for the morrow, or for a day in the next thousand years-in neither can we do anything, in both, God is doing everything."

(MacDonald) The future is not our domain. We are creatures created for the present. Yet because we each have eternity in our hearts, we cannot help but wonder about the future. Our future gaze is not a problem in and of itself; the problem is the delusion that we can control events in that far-off land, closed off to us until it becomes our present. Control is the root of our anxiety. We desire to control that which has not been placed in our hands. We live in the future, attempting to master it and bring it under our control. All the while, we are creating worry for ourselves, sowing seeds of anxiety into the soil of our souls. "Tomorrow makes today's whole head sick, its whole heart faint. When we should be still, sleeping or dreaming, we are fretting about an hour that lies a half sun's journey away!" (MacDonald)

If control is the root of anxiety, one must give up control to be free from fear. Here Jesus turns our attention to the most unlikely of teachers. He calls us to observe and learn from the birds of the air and flowers of the field. The birds and the flowers share a similar quality, a quality we shared before the fall, before we tried to usurp our creator and become creators ourselves. Unlike us, both the bird and the flower live eternally in the present; they are unworried or unbothered about the future. They have committed themselves wholly to the care of God by embracing the Holy Present. Only by living in the present can we make ourselves wholly available to the care of God. God is the Holy Present, the eternal I AM, the unmoved mover, the unchangeable, immutable first cause. He exists outside of time and knows all things in time. God is perfect peace because he is the eternal present. He forever is and will be, and he is inviting us to commit the future to him so that we might enjoy his holy present.

None of us could add an hour to our lives if we tried. All we can do is trust God here and now. God is eternally consistent, unlike the pagan gods whose moods were subject to change and as fickle as human emotions. He is not subject to change. He is always and ever-present. We need not fear the future or the things that lay outside our control because we can put our trust in the consistent character of God. We must learn to embrace the here and now and commit all our cares to God. Only then will we be free of our anxieties and worries. We must learn to leave the future to him and remember to be people of the Holy Present. This is what it means to seek his kingdom, to commit our whole lives, body, and soul to the righteous rule and reign of God. By placing ourselves in his care, we know that no matter what we face, we are anchored in him and need not fear, even in the face of death.

God and his peace are present to us through the gift of his Spirit. To walk in step with the Spirit requires we give up control and follow his leading. We are to be like Christ, who fully committed his life into the hands of the Father. But this isn't easy; it goes against every fiber of our being, so it takes discipline to give up control, exorcise or anx- iety and give in to the Holy Present. This doesn't happen overnight but must be cultivated like a seed till it takes root in our souls and becomes our reality.

IV. Learning to Live in the Holy Present

Learning to live in the Holy Present requires us to cede control when tempted to take the reins. We need a constant reminder that we are creatures of the present entrusted to the Father. This is accomplished through habits that continuously challenge our desire to control and daily put us before the Father so that we might trust in him like the Son. While this list isn't exhaustive, Stillness, Prayer, and Sabbath, in particular, help us to simultaneously cede control and remind us that we are creatures created for the Holy Present. While these practices often overlap, we must understand them isolated from one another because each has a unique power of its own when practiced with faith and alongside the Spirit's leading.

1. **Stillness**

"Be still, and know that I am God." (Psalm 46:JO)

We live in an age of perpetual motion. Even when seated, our minds are a million miles away as our social media feeds inundate us with content from across the globe. Attention spans are shorter, and our capacity to sit still lasts only for brief moments between computer screens. Yet stillness is vital to being human. To still be and enjoy the fact that we are, that we exist, is one of the greatest gifts God has given us. When we are still, we consider who we are and who we were created for. Movement is the enemy of revelation, and while God can speak in the hustle and bustle, his voice is often crowded out by our cares and concerns. Stillness invites us to enjoy, enjoy the breath we've been given, and glorify the one who breathed it into our being. When we sit still, we recognize we are not in control. In fact, by being still, we cede control and acknowledge that God is moving in ways we cannot comprehend or imagine.

2. **Prayer**

Do not worry about anything, but in everything by prayer and supplication with thanksgiving, let your requests be made known to God. 7 And the peace of God, which surpasses all understanding, will guard your hearts and your minds in Christ Jesus. (Philippians 4:5-7)

Prayer removes our cares and concerns from our hands and places them in the hands of God. Prayer doesn't turn us into apathetic drones, instead, it teaches us to say, "Your will be done on earth as it is in heaven." By faith, we know God's will is good, even when we cannot comprehend it. By praying, we cease "caring" and are free from the bonds of anxiety that bind us. When we are anxious, the best thing we can do, is turn our nervous rumblings into fervent prayer. Prayer places us firmly in the present by putting the future in God's care. When we feel like we are losing control, prayer reminds us that we are not in control and calls us to call on our Father to take the reins from our weary hands. So, "Pray, even [when] you feel nothing, see nothing. For when you are dry, empty, sick, or weak, at such a time is your prayer most pleasing to God, even though you may find little joy in it. This is true of all believing prayer." (St. Julian of Norwich)

3. Sabbath

The practice of the Sabbath has, for many, been lost. We are people of progress, movement, and innovation. The concept of surrendering a day to rest is a blasphemy of the worst kind. We are a people of doers and, by our doing, we desire to control our lives. As Abraham Heschel put it, "Life goes wrong when the control of space, the acquisition of things…becomes our sole concern." Sabbath reorients us away from the temporal, the forces of nature we hopelessly try to control, and fixes our attention on what is eternal, that is the Holy Present or, as Abraham Heschel calls it, a Cathedral in Time. The Sabbath frees us from the "tyranny of Space" and invites us to "turn from the results of creation to the mystery of creation." As we make this turn, we release our grip on our cares and cast them into the hands of God. By facing eternity, we once again embrace the Holy Present and place ourselves entirely into the loving care of the Father.

V. Close

Every day we are tasked with entrusting ourselves to the Father. We succeed far more than we hope and fail far more than we realize. There are no magic bullets in the Christian faith; there is only wrestling, the daily struggle of flesh and Spirit, what Tolkien called the Long Defeat. But there is hope, for there is one who wholly entrusted himself to the Father, even to the point of death. Jesus has done for us what we cannot do for ourselves. By embracing him, we welcome the Father and the peace he brings. And that peace, no soul-sucking demon can take away.

Let us Pray.

Father,
I give up control.
I embrace your Holy Present.
I cannot control the future,
I can do nothing about my past.
So, I commit myself to you,
for all I have is now, this moment here.
I place all my cares into your hands,
and like the birds, I worry not about what comes
but fully embrace what is.

Amen.

Ryan Diaz is a poet, lecturer, and theologian from Queens, NY. He holds a BA in History from St. Johns University and is currently completing a MA in Biblical Studies. Ryan's writing attempts to find the divine in the ordinary, the thin place where fantasy and reality meet. Ryan's work has been featured in the *Scribble Literary Journal*, *Ekstasis Magazine*, *Wingless Dreamer*, *In Parentheses*, *Tempered Rune Press* and *The Washington Institute*. He currently lives in Queens, NY with his wife Janiece.

GREG PETERS

Sermon for the Second Sunday of Easter 2020
Anglican Church of the Epiphany, La Mirada, CA

The supper at Emmaus in Luke 24:13-35 is one of my favorite texts in all of Holy Scripture. It is only found in Luke's Gospel (although there is a passing reference, it appears, to the event in Mark 16:12-13) but we are all the richer for having it. The narrative is straightforward in that two men are walking away from Jerusalem to the village of Emmaus. It is likely that these men were disciples of Jesus (though Luke does not say that explicitly) because they are aware of "all [the] things that had happened" (v. 18) in Jerusalem related to Jesus' death; they understand him to be "a prophet mighty in deed and word before God and all the people" (v. 19); and they thought (rightly, it turns out, but they do not know it yet) that Jesus would be "the one to redeem Israel" (v. 21). In fact, they are even aware of the resurrection, but they seem to think that it was something other than the resurrection -- that his body had been stolen by the Romans, perhaps. If they were disciples or followers of Jesus, they appear not to have fully understood Jesus' teaching regarding his death and resurrection. Had they understood it fully, it is hard to think that they would have left Jerusalem to go home to Emmaus. In any case, the resurrected, yet not-able-to-be-fully-seen Jesus joins them along the way and explains everything to them – "beginning with Moses and all the Prophets, he interpreted to them in all the Scriptures the things concerning himself" (v. 27).

Upon reaching Emmaus the two invite Jesus to "stay with [them]" (v. 29). Jesus agrees, they eat, and by eating "their eyes were opened, and they recognized him" (v. 31). So what does this eating have to do with seeing and coming to a knowledge of Jesus as the Messiah? To answer we must start with another question: What did they eat? Textually we are told that they ate blessed bread, but within the context of the Gospel of Luke, we know that they are eating the Body of Christ, for this eating is Eucharistic. In Luke's account of the feeding of the five thousand, we read, "And taking the five loaves and the two fish, [Jesus] looked up to heaven and said a blessing over [the loaves of bread]" (9:16a). Then, at the Last Supper (or the first Holy Eucharist), we read, "And [Jesus] took bread, and when he had given thanks, he broke it and gave it to them, saying, 'This is my body, which is given for you. Do this in remembrance of me'" (22:19). From this perspective we can see that the feeding of the five thousand looks ahead to the Eucharist, and now, in the Emmaus narrative, it looks back, serving as an inclusio. Thus the answer to the question, "What did they eat?" is the Holy Eucharist, that is, the Body of Christ. So what does this eating of the Holy Eucharist have to do with seeing and coming to a knowledge of Jesus as the Messiah?

Again, we take our lead from Jesus' feeding of the five thousand. Immediately after this event, Luke continues his Gospel this way: "Now it happened that as [Jesus] was praying alone, the disciples were with him. And he asked them, 'Who do the crowds say that I am?' And they answered, 'John the Baptist. But others say, Elijah, and others, that one of the prophets of old has risen.' Then he said to them, 'But who do you say that I am?' And Peter answered, 'The Christ of God'" (9:18-20). So the event that looks forward to the Eucharist is followed by a recognition of Jesus' Messianic identity and the event that looks back to the Eucharist includes a recognition of Jesus's Messianic identity. Partaking in the Holy Eucharist, then, brings us greater knowledge of the person of Jesus Christ, drawing us ever closer to he who is the Savior of the world. In the words of the fifth-century theologian Augustine of Hippo: "no one should doubt that his being recognized in the breaking of bread is the sacrament, which brings us together in recognizing him." And elsewhere, "The faithful… know Christ in the breaking of bread." But this "knowing" is not just cognitive: it concerns the heart. It is not just about knowing things that are visible: it is about knowing that which is only spiritually perceived.

Before eating the Holy Eucharist with Jesus, the two disciples' "eyes were kept from recognizing" Jesus (v. 16). This exact expression only occurs one other place in the Holy Scriptures, in Genesis 3:7a: "Then the eyes of both [Adam and Eve] were opened, and they knew that they were naked." In the way in which the eating from the Tree of the Knowledge of Good and Evil opened the eyes of Adam and Eve to sin, it helped them to see and recognize an up-until-that-moment hidden reality. The same is true for the Emmaus disciples: they now know Jesus is the Christ and all of the Law and the Prophets spoke of him, some- thing that is only spiritually perceived. In other words, Jesus is the new Adam. Wherein the first Adam fell and opened human eyes to sin, the new Adam defeats Satan and does not sin (Luke 1:1-11). Wherein the first Adam brings death, the new Adam gives food that brings sight, understanding and life.

The implication of this, then, seems obvious to me, and I imagine to you too. The Holy Eucharist is not just something that brings us together as the Church, giving evidence of our visible unity and catholicity, though it does that. It does more than that: it changes us individually, and in changing us individually, it changes us corporately. For in seeing Christ in all of his hidden glory by way of the Holy Eucharist, we run to tell others this Good News while our hearts burn within us (vv. 32-35). As we then partake today of this Holy Eucharist, may we too have our eyes opened to the truth of Jesus Christ in such a way that we run to tell others, bringing them into the Body of Christ, both eucharistically and ecclesially.

The Rev. Dr. Greg Peters is Rector of Anglican Church of the Epiphany, La Mirada, CA, as well as Professor of Medieval and Spiritual Theology in the Torrey Honors Institute at Biola University and Servants of Christ Research Professor of Monastic Studies and Ascetical Theology at Nashotah House Theological Seminary, WI. See his academic profile at https://www.biola.edu/directory/people/greg-peters.

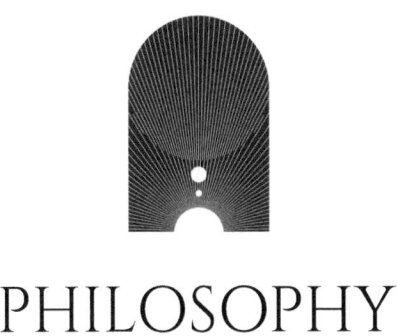

PHILOSOPHY

RILEY BOUNDS

The Necessity View as the Most Accurate Account of Metaphysical Relation in Physicalism

Introduction

In this paper, I will argue for the superiority of the Necessity View of physicalism over competing views in its account of the relation between instantiated properties and physical properties, that relation being metaphysical necessitation. I will contrast the Necessity View with two popular non-modal accounts of the relation between instantiated and physical properties: the Semantic View and the Identity View.[1] I will offer a brief explanation of why these views don't carry the same weight as the Necessity View for physicalism and explain how their non-modal assumptions undermine them.

Daniel Stoljar defines the Necessity View of physicalism as "the idea that physicalism is the view that every instantiated property is necessitated by some physical property."[2] The Necessity View is synonymous with necessitation physicalism, which is formulated thus: "Physicalism is true at w if and only if for every property F instantiated at w, there is some physical property G instantiated at w such that, for all possible worlds w^*, if G is instantiated at w^*, then F is instantiated at w^*."[3]

This view is not bound exclusively to necessitation by physical properties. It may well be that certain physical states, say the state of being in pain, are necessitated by a group of physical states of affairs,

---

1. Importantly, there is a subset of the Identity View called the Realization View, which is certainly worthy of discussion but cannot be explored in this paper due to space constraints. See Daniel Stoljar, *Physicalism* (New York: Routledge, 2010), 122-125.
2. Ibid, 110.
3. Ibid, 112.

not simply the necessitation of a physical property.[4] This version of physicalism doesn't preclude particulars either: a thing's having a physical property may necessitate a certain other physical property or state, say my own state of pain being necessitated by a physical thing's possessing a physical property.[5]

Like the Theory View and Starting Point View, the Necessity View isn't laying claim to the truth or falsity of physicalism; rather, it seeks to define what physicalism *is*. What distinguishes the Necessity View from the Theory and Starting Point Views is that it focuses on the relation between instantiated properties and physical properties; in other words, as the theory of physicalism holds that every instantiated property must be related in some way to physical properties, the Necessity View explains that the relation holding between instantiated properties and physical properties is one of metaphysical necessitation.[6]

The Necessity View vs. Competing Theories

Within the doctrine of physicalism, all theories of metaphysical relation between instantiated properties and physical properties seek to articulate why physical properties must bear relation to every property.[7] The main methodological difference between the Necessity View and competing views is the latter's articulation of physicalism in non-modal terms. The first competing view is what Stoljar calls the Semantic View, which holds that "physicalism is a thesis about meaning rather than about the nature of the world: it says that every statement or predicate is synonymous with some physical statement or predicate."[8] He goes on to clarify: "for physical properties, there are predicates of physical

---

4 Ibid, 113.
5 Ibid, 113-114.
6 Ibid, 110, 111.
7 Ibid, 117.
8. Ibid.

language which canonically express them."[9] The same would be true of psychological properties as predicates of a psychological language.[10] Foregoing the incoherency of physical predicate language, it would seem there are meaningful predicates that aren't synonymous with physical predicates, like the predicate "has a big heart" in the sentence "J. P. has a big heart" ("heart" here, of course, being the metaphor for soul or personality). There are many more problems with the Semantic View, but given its general vagueness, I think the rebuttal here will suffice to move on.[11]

The next view is the Identity View, which holds that "Physicalism is true at world w if and only if every property instantiated at w is identical to some physical property instantiated at w."[12] So on this view, we're back to dealing with physicalism as a proper matter, not simply the meanings of predicates. Essentially, the view holds that every property must somehow be identical to a physical property.[13] But the Identity View still comes up short with the problem of multiple realization. Stoljar uses the psychological property of wondering if it will rain soon to show that it's logically coherent that beings in other possible worlds might have the same thought without being able to instantiate the exact same physical property since that is what the Identity Views requires. There's more to be said, but already the Identity View has proven lacking in comparison to the Necessity View.[14]

Why Metaphysical Necessitation?

In the end, the non-modal assumptions of these two views inhibit them rather than help. As Stoljar says, "any thesis that has a chance of

---

9. Ibid.
10. Ibid.
11. See Stoljar 118 for further examination.
12. Ibid, 118.
13. Ibid, 118-119.
14. Ibid, 118-119.

deserving the name 'physicalism' will at least have to entail (something like) the thesis that every property is necessitated by a physical property."[15] It would be tempting for the physicalist to dispense with metaphys- ical necessity altogether given its modal nature. One might wish to couch the relation between instantiated and physical properties solely in a thesis of the actual world, not in possible worlds, in an effort to sim- plify things. But physicalism isn't content to stay within the confines of the natural sciences; it goes on to make more sweeping philosophical claims of what is possible and what's not. Thus physicalism opens itself up to critique in its appropriation and use of modality, and the tools of critique are possible world semantics.[16]

Bibliography
    Stoljar, Daniel. Physicalism. New York: Routledge, 2010.

---

15 Ibid, 129.
16 Ibid.

Riley Bounds is Cofounder, Publisher, and Editor in Chief of Solum Press. He holds an MA in Philosophy from Talbot School of Theology at Biola University and a BA in Creative Writing from the University of Central Oklahoma. He is a poet and fiction writer. His work has appeared in *Earth and Altar Magazine*, *Ekstasis Magazine*, *Amethyst Review*, *Heart of Flesh Literary Journal*, *This Present Former Glory: An Anthology of Honest Spiritual Literature*, and *Saccharine Poetry*, among others. His debut chapbook, *Hands of Years*, is forthcoming from Alabaster Leaves Publishing. He hopes to pursue doctoral study and work in ministry.

JOHN J. BRUGALETTA

The Concept of Evil

There is a web site that is open to questions of any variety, and then allows almost anyone to answer the question. Such was the case with the question, "What is the strongest argument against the existence of God?" The person who chose to reply said only, "The fact that there is evil in the world," implying by the brevity of his or her answer that the case was now closed (as it is for some philosophers). It interests me that a person who believes there is no God should choose the word "evil," for the word is meaningful only when uttered by someone who does not confuse sorrows with the utter absence of good.

And this confusion is not only difficult to avoid by the human race, it is almost impossible. Even Voltaire, that brilliant man, was shocked (though probably not personally inconvenienced) that a benevolent God should allow the widely destructive 1755 earthquake in Lisbon, Portugal. Again and again, when war costs many lives, or infants die, or pandemics threaten the survival of millions, the word evil is either applied or implied.

My point here is not that these should be passed over like missing a meal; it is that we, with our limited knowledge and wisdom, are not competent to apply the word evil to anything in our experience, especially when a cosmic force is implied.

Consider the following illustration. A toddler watches while her father buries her dead guinea pig in the family rose bed. The father, sensing the child's grief, tells her that the animal will turn into a rose one day (as it would, in a sense). But the toddler, having no knowledge of plant growth, says, "You're not telling me the truth." Because her extreme youth gave her no way to understand her father's statement, she assumed that his attempt at consolation was a lie. And this case is parallel with that of many adults who speak of evil while having only a limited grasp of this complex problem.

Did we know, for example, that those who have made a study of the concept of evil have found it necessary to divide the examples into two types, a broad concept and a narrow concept? And then, with evil in the broad sense, there are again two types, natural evil and moral evil. And this is only an offhand look at a widespread field of study.

But even a superficial knowledge of religions will allow one to see that, among the three main faiths (Judaism, Christianity and Islam), only Christianity faces this problem called theodicy. It is only in Christianity that Christ's behavior and words are taken as true guides to the nature of God, and his nature turns out to be omniscient, omnipotent and benevolent. It is because of human interpretations of these three superlative and unimaginable traits that many afflicted people think there is no God at all. It seems to never occur to them that if God is omniscient, we creatures with inferior minds may never understand what happens in that extravagant and incomparable mind.

It is not an irrelevancy that the book of James cautions against there being many teachers, for a conscientious teacher must not only know a great deal, but must also be keenly aware of his or her relative lack of knowledge. It was this awareness of his own shortcomings that caused Socrates to puzzle over what the Oracle of Delphi said about him: that he was the wisest man in Athens. Finally he decided that, because everyone else claimed to know much though clearly did not, he was indeed the wisest because he knew that he did not know. Human wisdom is not so much a conquest as it is a lifelong search.

John J. Brugaletta is Professor Emeritus at California State University, Fullerton, where he taught courses in Shakespeare, Dante, Homer and C. S. Lewis. He has published essays on "Forgiving as Process," "C. S. Lewis on the Wait [sic] of Glory," and "The Merchant of Venice."

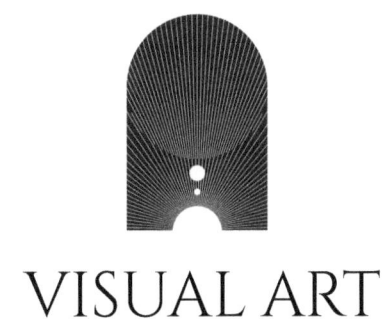

VISUAL ART

CYNTHIA SOWERS

Studies after Giovanni Battista Tiepolo,
St. Jerome in the Desert, I

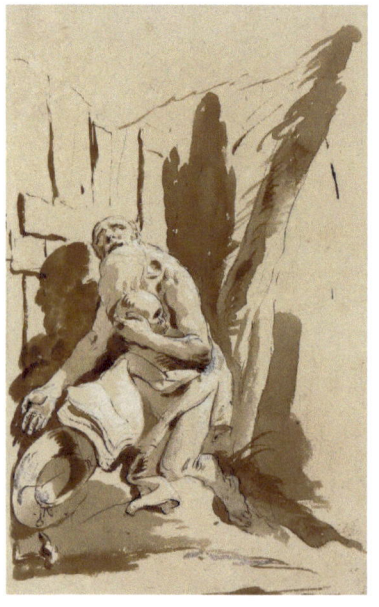

Tiepolo, *St. Jerome Penitent,* c. 1720s. Pen & brown ink, brown & white wash, black chalk on paper, 1.73" x 1.16". Art Gallery of South Australia.

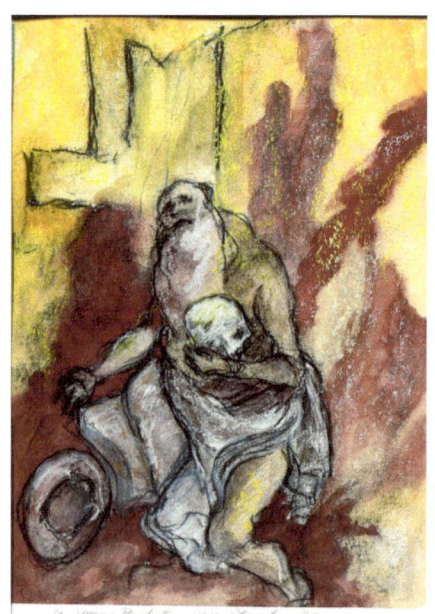

SowerS, *St. Jerome Penitent, after Tiepolo,* 2018. Water Color and Conté Crayon on Paper, 12" x 8".

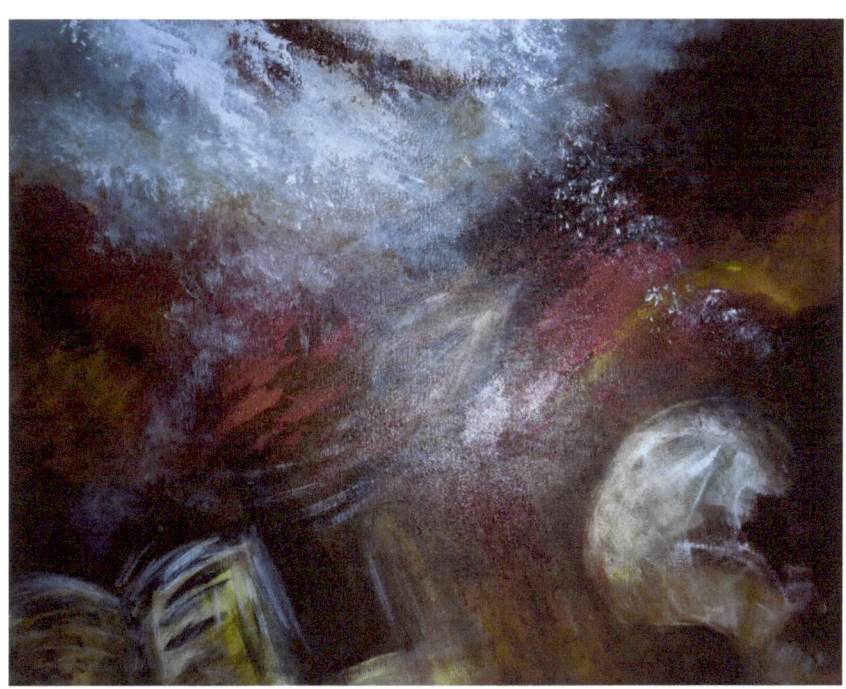

SowerS, *St. Jerome Penitent,* 2018. Acrylic on Canvas 15" x 20".

Studies after Giovanni Battista Tiepolo, II
St. Jerome Listens to the Angels in the Desert

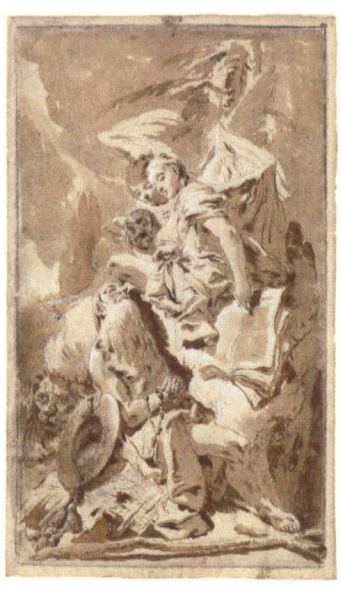
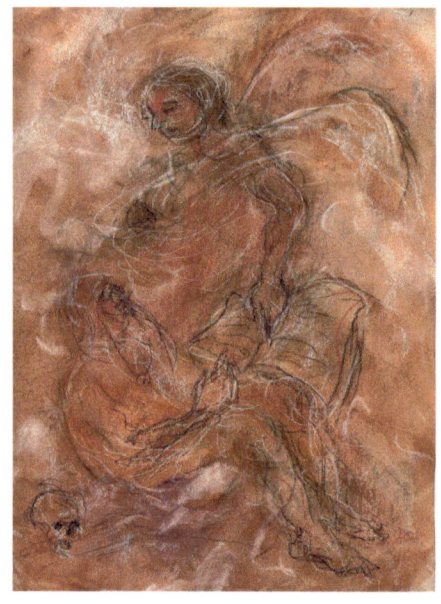

Tiepolo, *St. Jerome Listens to the Angels in the Desert*, c. 1732. Pen and brown ink with brown wash over black chalk, heightened with thick white gouache; ruled black chalk borders, on laid paper; 17" x 10". The Armand Hammer Collection.

Sowers, *St. Jerome Listens to the Angels in the Desert after Tiepolo*, 2020. Watercolor and conté crayon on canvas, 13" x 8".

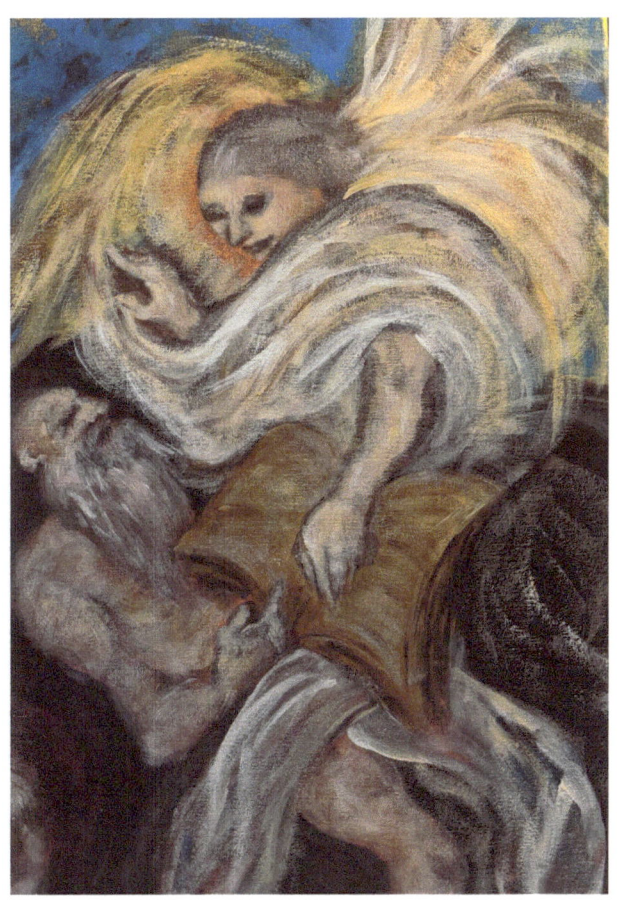

Sowers, *St. Jerome Listens to the Angels in the Desert, after Tiepolo*, 2020. Acrylic on Canvas, 20" x 15".

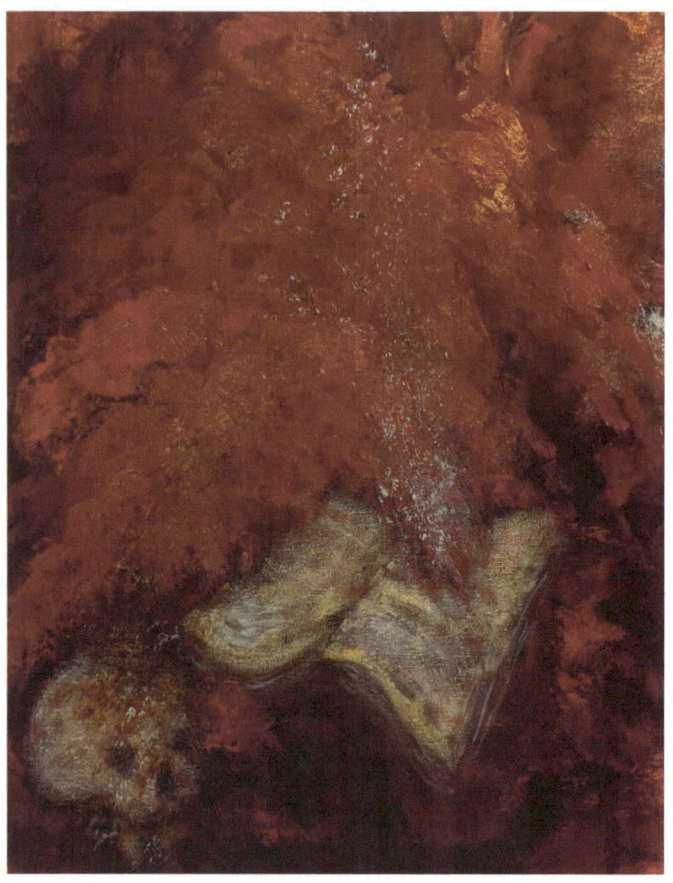

Sowers, *Skull, Book, and Angel*, 2021. Acrylic on canvas 20" x 15".

Cynthia Sowers was a Senior Lecturer at the Residential College of the University of Michigan. Until her retirement in 2019, she developed and taught interdisciplinary courses for the Arts and Ideas in the Humanities Program. Her past teaching and current creative activity is centered on the engagement of literature and the visual arts.

www.ingramcontent.com/pod-product-compliance
Lightning Source LLC
Chambersburg PA
CBHW041947240526
45473CB00036B/2406